THE EXISTENTIALIST POSTURE

THE EXISTENTIALIST POSTURE

by ROGER LINCOLN SHINN

A Christian look at its meaning, impact, values, dangers

REVISED EDITION

ASSOCIATION PRESS   New York

THE EXISTENTIALIST POSTURE

Copyright © 1970, 1959 by

National Board of Young Men's Christian Associations

———

Association Press, 291 Broadway, New York, N.Y. 10007

Standard Book Number:
Hardbound Edition: 8096-1778-1
Paperback Edition: 8096-1763-3

Library of Congress Catalog Card Number: 77-93426

Printed in the United States of America

CONTENTS

Preface

Chapter   *Page*

1. In the Air, in Our Bones   9

2. A Basic Clash   13

    Two Kinds of Meaning   13
    Essence and Existence   17
    The Need for Two Postures   21

3. The Existentialist Revolt   29

    Threats to Selves   30
    Beginnings of Rebellion   35
    Existentialism Arrives   37

4. The Disturbing Dane   43

    The Critique of Rationalism   45
    Self-Discovery   48
    The Leap of Faith   52
    The Attack upon Christendom   54

5. The Fractured Family   57

    The Great Divide   57
    The "Death of God"   59
    Twentieth-Century Atheism   62
    Atheists and Saints   71

6. Directions of Faith   73

    Catholic Objectivity and
       Existentialism   75
    Judaism and *I-Thou*   78
    Existential Protestantism   81

7. Voices, Sights, and Deeds   91

    Indirect Communication   91
    The Verbal Arts   93
    The Theater   98
    The Visual Arts and Music   101
    Tamed Existentialism   104
    A New Age of Protest   106

8. Some Existential Judgments   111

    Notes by Chapters   117

    For Further Reading   123

PREFACE

THE TENTH BIRTHDAY of *The Existentialist Posture* requires a decision. The past decade has been a pell-mell period in history. "For me," wrote Jean-Paul Sartre in his autobiographical book, *The Words,* "speed is measured not so much by the distance covered as by the power of uprooting." A lot has been uprooted in recent years.

This book was initially intended to be a book of its time. On re-reading it I have found pages I am willing to stand by and others that tell me how much things have changed. Occasionally I have even felt a bit of nostalgia, as no true existentialist should do. The book, I saw, was ready for either retirement or revision.

Writers, it is an open secret, crave appreciation. I am one of the clan at that point. I am grateful that people have told me the book is helpful, that some who have read it in Arabic and Turkish translations say it has been useful in their societies. So when the publisher suggested that the use of the book justified a revised edition, I quickly agreed to have a go at it. Here is the result, the basic structure the same, but the contents considerably modified and up-dated.

It is still a short, introductory book that bypasses a lot of the intricacies in an immensely intricate subject. I hope that it helps some readers to get their feet wet, so that they will then want, in a characteristic phrase of Kierkegaard, to venture far out.

Roger L. Shinn

ONE
IN THE AIR, IN OUR BONES

NOBODY CAN TELL YOU exactly what existentialism is. Anybody who claims he can is a fraud. Some things you have to discover for yourself.

One great emphasis of existentialism is that there is something phony about concepts, that clarity is deceptive, that life cannot be bounded and defined—and existentialism deals with life. Experience includes the chaotic, the unfathomable, the absurd; and these cannot be imprisoned in formal definitions or even in entire books.

Still it is possible to talk about existentialism and the experiences that give rise to it. It is possible to communicate some of its themes and something of its color and smell. That is what I aim to do in an introductory sort of way, in this book.

It might be convenient if I could start with the question, "What is existentialism?," and then produce a definition. But I have already denied myself that privilege—or, rather, existentialism has denied it to me.

I can do a little better with the question, "Who is an existentialist?" But that question has its problems too. If you go around asking people, "Are you an existentialist?," only a phony will answer, "Yes." The real existentialist is likely to give you the brush-off. He is frequently rude. He is not much interested in people who want to know about existentialism. He *is* interested in the person who has bumped into some disturbing experience or has met some shock that makes him ask, "What am I doing, anyhow?" Specifically, he does not want to identify himself as one of the category of people known to classifiers as existentialists. He wants to be himself.

Hence there's no automatic way to identify the existentialist. He may be wearing blue jeans and a beard, beating bongo drums in jazz time. He may be a scholar and philosopher, sophisticated and caustic, denouncing tradition and religion. He may be a theologian, telling the story of Abraham and Isaac or the story of Jesus Christ. He may be a soldier, a poet, a man at prayer.

Existentialism can be a bewildering affair. Some people trace its history (too glibly) in terms of two leaps: first, from the cafés and nightclubs of left-bank Paris to comparable spots in New York's Greenwich Village; then from New York (via a few art galleries, theaters, and college campuses) to Hollywood, then back again to the rebellious campuses. But others find it running from Socrates and the Old Testament to contemporary times.

A few people study existentialism in some of the weightiest philosophical books of this and the past generation. Others pick up their information and their clues from popular magazines, the Sunday supplement of the newspaper, or the theater of the absurd.

But most people—those who know all about ex-

istentialism and those who know nothing about it
—have felt its influence. Cosmic rays affect us all,
whether or not we have heard of them; and existentialism, like cosmic rays, is in the air. And it's
in our bones. It has caught up one mood of our
present world, and it has helped to create that
mood.

So, though some call it a philosophy, others feel
its impact far from the world of scholars. It produces novels with strange names like *Nausea* and
more dignified names like *The Stranger.* Theater
and film occasionally express it deliberately, more
often communicate it indirectly. Painting and
scholarship, politics and religion are different because of it. The progressive education of most
American schools has a tinge of it. If much of its
vocabulary is for the eggheads, its main concerns
are life and experience in this magnificent, crazy,
overpowering age of history. So the popular arts,
even advertising, spread its message (or messages,
or intimations of messages) widely. And the comic
strip *Pogo* has been called "existentialism for the
masses." (Maybe it shouldn't have been called
that, since existentialism is concerned with in-
dividuals, not masses.)

But the minute anybody tries to pin down existentialism he finds out how kaleidoscopic and con-
troversial it is. A puzzled actress, who thought her
career depended on finding out enough about it to
play the role of an existentialist, learned from a
professor that it was "free love and futility." If she

had asked a clergyman, he might have told her that it was one of the most powerful of theological movements. Both answers have some factual justification.

Back in the 1940's the Vatican put on its "Index of Prohibited Books" (now abolished) the writings of Jean-Paul Sartre, the most prominent of the French "atheistic existentialists." But "atheistic" Russia in those days also banned his writings, presumably for different reasons. Many conservatives put Sartre on their private "Indexes," because they thought he was playing the communist game. At some American universities, however, campus Christian groups produced his plays because they raised fundamental religious issues.

Sartre must have enjoyed all this. He did not want to fit into anybody's categories; he aimed to upset the categories.

If the evidence of truth is a "clear and distinct idea," as philosopher and mathematician René Descartes once maintained, I cannot tell you the truth about existentialism. Certainly I cannot fit into any available pigeonhole anything so fertile, so diverse, so intense. What I intend to do is describe some of the major motifs of the movement and tell something of its story.

TWO
A BASIC CLASH

PEOPLE NEVER FIND IT EASY to understand themselves and their world. But they keep trying. Myth and poetry, astronomy and chemistry, religion and painting, medicine and philosophy—all are explorations in understanding. All help. None is ever complete.

In the venture of understanding one precious achievement is *objectivity*. Without objectivity our prejudices get between us and the facts. Or our emotions interfere with calm reasoning. Or the few facts that concern *us* appear more important than the many facts that affect *the world*. Painful experience teaches us to distrust the judgments of people who cannot be objective, and even of ourselves at times when we cannot be objective.

Objectivity is a trait that goes with maturity, with civilization. It makes possible great achievements in knowledge. But *objectivity sometimes prevents understanding*. The limitations of objectivity produce existentialism.

Two Kinds of Meaning

To get at this issue, look at a series of propositions. They all deal with the same subject, but in vastly different ways.

1. All men are mortal. That has been a favorite proposition of logicians for centuries. They like it because it is one of the few general (or all-inclusive) statements about men or anything else that will not start an argument. (Note: The proposition says nothing about immortality. It means only that all men come to an end of their earthly careers, that this present life moves inevitably toward death.) A teacher can write the sentence on the blackboard or an author can put it in a book, and everyone assents. No one can *quite* prove the statement; of all the people who have ever lived, about three and a half billion have not died. But on the time-scale of history they are all young— say, under 200 years, to make a safe estimate— and we expect them to die. So the evidence for the proposition is so overwhelming that nobody reasonably disagrees.

The proposition concerns *objective fact.* You may dislike it, resent it, wish it were not so. But you accept it, pretty much as a matter of course, usually without a wail or a shudder.

Now compare that proposition with a second one.

2. You are going to die today. Suppose the statement comes from someone who knows—your doctor or jailer or platoon leader in battle. It comes with convincing authority, and you believe it.

That proposition, logically, is simply one of the many cases that enter into Proposition No. 1. The minute you recognized that "all men are mortal," you knew that you would die sometime. Now you know when. That detail is not very important to logic or mankind.

But Proposition No. 2 has a completely different ring from No. 1. It strikes a blow. Whether you
resist or welcome the blow, it changes you. Were
you eager for a vacation or fearful of a debt coming due? Were you expecting to take out more
insurance? Such acts look different now. You no
longer have the investment in the future that you
once had. Your *existence* is at stake. Death is now
an *existential* concern.

In a way Proposition No. 2 is far less important
than No. l. It concerns only one of the three and
a half billion people on earth. But it has far more
power. Even so, it can be made still more potent.

*3. "Fool! This night your soul is required of
you."* The language has now shifted, and so has
the speaker. It is God who says this, at the end of
a parable of Jesus (Luke 12:20, RSV).

The story tells of a rich man, who exults that he
must pull down his barns and build bigger ones to
hold his goods. He congratulates himself: "Soul,
you have ample goods laid up for many years; take
your ease, eat, drink, be merry." Then God deliv-
ers the blow: "Fool! This night your soul is required of you; and the things you have prepared,
whose will they be?"

Here is more than a notification of death. It is
a call to a reckoning. To some it carries the meaning of a judgment before God. And even someone
who disbelieves in God is likely to sense in it a
portentous challenge to all his accomplishments

and purposes. To any sensitive person it is intensely painful to think that his life has possibly been worthless. The call to add up his deeds and show that the sum is not *zero* demands that he search himself with "fear and trembling."

Now recall the three propositions. No. 1 may interest you. It is general and objective. No. 2—if you hear and believe it—may jar you. It concerns your physical existence and all that you associate with that. No. 3—again if you hear and believe it —can shatter. It thrusts not merely at *biological existence* but at the *meaning of personal existence.*

In much modern literature and thinking, the word existence has come to take that latter meaning. (Sometimes the German form, *Existenz,* is used.) *Existentialism* is the outlook that starts from *personal existence.* Although it may go in many directions, it begins by asking what it means to be a self. It questions every person about his decisions, about the purpose and nature of his own existence.

Existentialism says that persons discover some truth, not by cultivating objectivity, but by entering into the intensity of personal experience. Involvement rather than detachment may be the key to insight. A great deal of information about death (just to continue the example I have been using) comes from biochemists, insurance actuaries, and undertakers. But a deeper meaning comes to the person who learns what the death of himself or a friend does to his aims and his achievements.

There are other ways to describe the movement from Proposition No. 1 to No. 3 (with No. 2 as a halfway station). It is the turning from *the objective* to *the personal,* from *the general* to *the particular,* from *the abstract* to *the concrete*. It is the shift from *observation* to *involvement,* from *information* to *responsibility.*

But in all these contrasts, we must notice, existentialism does not run away from objectivity into subjectivity, at least as we normally use those terms. It is not interested in fantasies and wishful thinking. Selfhood, events that require choices, death—these are as objective as anything. They have their brutal factuality which no one can escape. But these objective realities disclose meanings to selves who meet them in personal concern. To crush such concern for the sake of detached knowledge may be to distort the apprehension of truth. And it may result, not in a greater mind, but in a more anemic self.

Essence and Existence

Another way to come at the issue and to get at its vocabulary is to use a distinction that philosophy has often used: the distinction between essence and existence. This style of thinking has led to some extremely intricate (and sometimes useless) literature, but the basic issue is fairly simple and important.

In any day's living you meet far more sense impressions than you can possibly count or take note of. You have developed a system for screening out many of them so that they don't catch your attention. You have also developed a system for organizing them and fitting them into your conceptual world. An infant learns to do this. By the time he can talk he has achieved a complex conceptual scheme. Instead of responding to sheer sense impressions, his mind and nervous system organize sensations so that he recognizes, not simply light and color (to mention only visual sensations), but cars, people, sidewalks, cats, dogs, dolls, coats, and so on. All this involves a process of classification and the ability to distinguish one class of things from others.

This ability to classify is a great help to clear thinking. It gets the number of objects in experience down to manageable proportions and changes our apprehension of the world from chaos to understanding. We look at a grassy plot without bothering our minds about its millions of bits of vegetation. For some purposes it's enough to know that it's grass rather than mud. For other purposes we may want to know that it is a mix of blue grass, rye grass, clover, dandelions, crabgrass, and buckhorn. In either case we are not giving attention to every last organism; we are classifying. We know that no two blades of grass are identical, but most of the time we don't care. The difference is unimportant, but the difference between blue grass and crabgrass may be impor-

tant. We may say, to use a long-established ter-
minology, that blue grass and crabgrass are *essen-
tially* different, which is to say they are different
in *essence.*

Take another example. There is a difference
between a lion and a fox, and the difference sometimes matters. But it requires some care to state
the difference accurately. We may start with the
fact that lions are bigger than foxes—except that
some large foxes are bigger than some baby lions.
We may say that lions are more dangerous (to
men if not to mice) than foxes, but a ravenous and
rabid fox might on occasion be more dangerous
than a well-fed and sleepy lion. In some particular
case a battle-scarred fox might not have a tail, but
that fact tells us nothing about the difference between foxes and lions. Apart from all the inciden-
tal differences in various specific cases, there are
essential differences—one of which is that lions
beget lions, not foxes. That distinction gets at the
essence of the case.

Part of man's intellectual and scientific progress comes from his ability to get away from ir-
relevant incidentals and to get at essentials.
Arithmetic deals with numbers and gets the same
answers, whether the numbers refer to rocks or to
people. Geometry works out the laws of spheres
quite apart from the fact that a sphere may be the
sun or a baseball. Physiology as a scientific discipline is more interested in the functioning of the
human heart than in the condition of my heart.
Psychology on some levels, gives more attention

to the more-or-less uniform processes of conditioned reflexes than to my unique personality.

All this, I repeat, is part of man's greatness. Without the ability to classify, to abstract, to screen out incidentals and get to the essence of things, he would live in confusion. He would be uncivilized, less than human.

But now a warning is appropriate. Our most elemental experiences are specific, and we can wrap these specifics up in generalizations only at the cost of losing something. Concepts are achieved by abstraction, but reality is concrete. The functional usefulness of classification does not take account of the immense variety of unique individual things. The uniformities that fascinate science and most philosophy are not the diversities that mark immediate experience. In short, essence is not existence.

Existentialists call attention to *existence*. They revel in the immediacy of experience, the richness of a world of unique occasions, the dazzling variety of life. They pay as much attention to direct sense experience as to mental concepts, as much to feeling as to rationality, as much to art as to science. They know—most of them, most of the time—the values of the scientific intellect; they think it is deceptive if it is taken to be the truth, the *whole* truth, and nothing but the truth.

More particularly the existentialist is concerned with *personal existence.* Sometimes he may even say that only persons exist: objects are, people exist. But whether or not he cultivates that peculiar vocabulary, the existentialist insists that personal existence is to be an individual, to will, to decide, to understand oneself, to make commitments, to live responsibly, to be involved rather than detached.

The Need for Two Postures

Obviously everyone takes the existential outlook at times. No one regards his own family simply as data for intellectualization. The most abstruse scholars, the most assiduous collectors of information are, before everything else, persons.

But equally obviously, no one lives in existential concern all the time. Sometimes people just get tired and don't care. At other times they cultivate the discipline of objectivity in order to attain their goals.

There is thus an existential impulse and an objective impulse in everyone. Some people incline one way, some the other. But it is impossible to divide the world into two groups of people, whom we might call existentialists and objectivists. Most people would not fit either group solely.

Instead we might say that existentialism and objectivity are two postures that we assume in our living. Both are necessary in life—whether for survival or fullness of life. The relating of the two is one of the most difficult things anyone does. It is the business of becoming a person, of conducting a life, of entering into selfhood.

Some examples will show the contribution of

each—of *existence* (in the special meaning I have been using) and of *objectivity:*

A first example is Socrates of ancient Athens. As the rigorous debater, concerned with exact definitions of terms, he was one of the pioneers in semantics and objective *philosophical reasoning.* But as the "gadfly" of the city, upsetting cherished prejudices and stirring up the public with his relentless questioning, he was a forerunner of the existentialists.

Both sides of his character came out during the last days of his life. In prison, condemned to die because of some conniving rascals and a biased jury, he talked with his friends. He wanted to discuss immortality. He presented several reasons for his belief that the soul does not die, and he asked his friends to search his logic for flaws. Naturally they did not want to argue. It is not very gentlemanly to tell a doomed man that his belief in immortality is false. But Socrates insisted. So determined was he to avoid subjective bias and wishful thinking that he preferred to be proved wrong—if he was wrong—than to die with a comforting belief. That kind of objectivity is one of the glorious achievements of philosophy.

Today some people accept the arguments of Socrates. But many find an event of his last hours more persuasive. The friends who visited him had bribed the jailors and arranged for Socrates to escape. All he had to do was walk out and leave town. But he refused. He had been condemned for his teaching. He still believed in that teaching and wanted to stick by it, at the cost of death, rather than run out. Besides, he was not afraid to die.

Socrates' arguments were his objective attempt to answer death. His refusal to run away was his existential answer. *Objectivity* asks whether life continues after death. *Existence* meets death confidently. There is a big difference between the two. We recognize it every now and then in people who believe with their minds in eternal life but are scared to death of dying.

I have referred often to death in this chapter because it is a prominent subject in the literature of existentialism. Again and again the issues of the meaning of life come up when a person faces death. But there are many other examples, and it is time to turn to a very different one.

A second example is not a person but a human enterprise: *science.* I have already touched upon it. Certainly science is one of the great monuments to the power of objective thinking. Scientific inquiry demands accuracy and honesty, with no concessions to prejudice. The laboratory has no place for the investigator who wants to nudge the calipers just a little or slip some acid into the test tube without recording it, in order to make the experiment agree with his subjective desires. Science overthrows hallowed authorities, blasts superstitions, derides subjectivity.

After many triumphs in the study of physical nature, science has begun to inquire into the behavior of society and persons. The techniques of objective inquiry have taught us things about ourselves that we did not know and preferred not to believe. And they will probably continue to teach us much more.

Just here, however, existentialism gives a warning. It says that only persons can understand personal behavior. It insists that experiments can deceive experimenters who do not know themselves. And, as the great Jewish existentialist Martin Buber taught, we do not know ourselves (or even become selves) except as we enter into truly personal relations with other people. If experimentation leads us to see other people only as objects to push around in the laboratory, it will fool us, perhaps destroy our own genuine selfhood.

Here is one of the most critical areas in which the objective and existential postures confront each other today. *Objectivity* says that the rats in the mazes tell us something about ourselves; *existence* says that they tell us falsehoods if they make us miss the glory and despair of personal life in personal relations.

There is no logical reason why both postures cannot point to truth. But to relate them truthfully is, again, not easy. Thus far our generation has not had much success in reaching an understanding of selves which is both scientifically and personally adequate.

There is, however, no necessary conflict between science and existentialism. Blaise Pascal, for instance, was one of the great pioneers of modern mathematics and physics, and at the same time the leading forerunner of modern existentialism. When a Jesuit Aristotelian argued against his scientific beliefs, Pascal answered with experiments. Neither church authority nor Aristotle's metaphysics could determine scientific fact. But with equal passion he insisted that no one can understand human beings unless he explores his own heart, with its mysteries beyond measurement and its secrets beyond objective determination.

A third example is *religion.* Although people may change their religious beliefs because of discussion, no one ever became religious simply by logical analysis. Religion releases and directs powerful emotions. It concerns worship, trust, dedication, commitment.

Every now and then someone lets go the idea that religion should be strictly a matter of personal feeling, with no reasoning at all. But that proposal never gets very far. Religion, uncriticized by reason, can produce snake handling, alcoholic fantasies, superstitions, crazed hallucinations. So, in every society, people must do some thinking about their religion.

So the human mind, via common sense and via philosophy and theology, thinks about religion. It attempts to bring some order into the experiences of men, to make distinctions between truth and falsehood. It seeks some rational clarity in matters of faith.

Sometimes it goes on to produce great theological systems. In the Middle Ages, for instance, such a system was called a *Summa,* because it tried to *sum up* man's knowledge of God and religious truth. Some of the systems aimed at great rational objectivity. They might try to prove the existence of God and the immortality of the soul, apart from any venture of faith. The arguments became abstruse and complicated.

Then came the existential protest. "By living, by dying, by being damned one becomes a theologian," said Martin Luther, "—not by understanding, reading, and speculating."[1] The point of religion, he insisted, was trust in God, not argument about God.

Luther did not want to destroy objectivity. Quite the contrary. He knew that some people live, die, and are damned without becoming theologians. He knew that religious passion is not the same thing as theological competence. He promoted schooling and translated the Scriptures in order that people might study and understand rather than accept in blind faith. But he declared with all the power of his mighty personality that there can be no religion apart from personal commitment, no faith that is not trust.

In religion, then, *objectivity* asks: Is there a God? *Existence* asks: What and whom can I trust? *Objectivity* asks: Why is there suffering and evil in the world? *Existence* asks: How shall I suffer? What shall I do about the evil in the world and the

---

[1] All footnotes appear under "Notes by Chapters," beginning on page 106.

sin within me?

In all these examples we see some consistent themes of the existentialist. He reiterates—pointedly and often impolitely—that a great deal of our objectivity is a pompous fraud. Whenever we point to the data of inquiry, he points to the inquirer. Whenever we mention a thought, he asks about the thinker. And he tells us that in reality there are no pure inquirers and thinkers. There are persons, who inquire and think, but who also hope and fear and make decisions.

Every belief (including emphatically his own belief), he says, tells us something about the believer. A man's personal commitments are part of the truth or falsity he declares. His anxieties, his cravings, his loves and lusts, his fear and despair, are as much a part of his truth as anything he perceives. He never simply recognizes truth; he decides what he will do and be, and his decision determines the truth he is capable of recognizing.

Not everyone agrees. Some hurl back the questions: "What has my guilt or ambition to do with the multiplication table, my decision to do with the structure of the uranium atom?"

And the existentialist says: "Not much. But if you choose to center your life (which is something different from learning to multiply) in the multiplication table, *that* is your decision. It is a stupid decision, because no one can center his life in digits. It is an evasive decision, probably an attempt to walk out on more difficult problems that haunt

you (as they haunt everyone). In so far as you
succeed, you doom yourself to become a cramped
and empty self. If you think that the multiplication table constitutes reality, you are a fool. *Your
decision* is a greater part of *your reality* than your
ability to manipulate numbers."

THREE
THE EXISTENTIALIST REVOLT

EXISTENTIALISM IS CONTEMPORARY. Not so long ago it was the latest thing. Although past the fad stage, it is still developing new forms. Some people practice its idiom, or revise it or invent new idioms, to show that they are *avant-garde.*

But, I have been saying, the existential posture is as old as human experience. All people have their existential moments. And many great characters of history have thought in vividly existential terms. The myths of ancient societies are mostly built around existential themes. The Bible throbs with existential power. (That is the trouble with the Bible, say some rationalists.) Often it is said that the Hebrews were characteristically existential, in contrast to the Greeks who cultivated objective reason. But we have seen the powerful existential bent in Socrates. Increasingly scholars are discovering a similar stance in other great Greek thinkers.

Repeatedly through Western history the existential drive has reasserted itself. Sometimes personal crisis, sometimes social turmoil, sometimes the Bible have stimulated it. The Protestant Reformation was one such occasion. Martin Luther was surely one of the most passionately existential of all men. Readers still misinterpret Luther and Calvin by turning their existential confessions into abstract systems.

If the posture is so old and so perennial, why did

29

history wait until recent times for the birth—or the eruption—of the "ism"? Why have the nineteenth and twentieth centuries developed the recognizable movement with a name and a literature?

The answer lies in the events and movements of modern history. Blindly, but as effectively as if by deliberate plan, a series of changes brought in the modern world. They came with drum beating and the offer of emancipation from the slavery of the past. Their effect, in practice, was often to steal from man his freedom. Sometimes they lured people, sometimes battered them, into something less than selfhood.

Threats to Selves

Because these movements still threaten lives today, it will pay to inspect some of them and to analyze their impact.

Threat No. 1. Man is a computer. Recently an electronic machine has been taught to play chess well enough to beat fairly good human players. Such machines far excel persons in solving some kinds of problems. Occasionally someone argues, with quite straight face, that the computer is a better machine than the human machine. Man, it appears, no longer makes decisions and shapes his destiny. He is a mechanism within the cosmic mechanism.

That story started a few centuries ago when a group of brilliant scientists—Copernicus, Kepler,

Galileo, Pascal, and Newton, among others—discovered methods of correlating factual observations with mathematical formulas in order to describe and predict the processes of nature. They revised our picture of the universe and gave the human race new powers.

They were rightly impressed with the potentiality of mathematics. Some of them (called mathematical rationalists) concluded that the universe is a vast machine. One of these was the French genius of the seventeenth century, René Descartes, who discovered analytic geometry. It is stylish these days to blame Descartes for all that has gone wrong in modern rationalism. That is unfair, but he is as good a symbol of the trouble as anyone.

Descartes asked the deep question: What is the place of persons in this great machine-universe? His answer was that human beings are the thinkers who figure out how the machine ticks. And he came up with a remarkable definition of the self, a definition which is both clearly true and utterly foolish: "I am a thing that thinks."[1]

Obviously everyone thinks—we hope. But no one has to say, "I am a thing that thinks." One might just as well say, "I am a thing that eats." Or, "I am a thing that struggles." Or, as some modern novelists (and a few of the existentialists) seem to say, "I am a thing that stinks." But one can say, "I am a *self* who hopes and fears, who loves and despises, who exists in anxiety and decision."

But the vogue was to define the self as a thinker, often (with a narrowing of Descartes' broad conception of thought) as a computer. Personality was on the way to becoming a rather inefficient machine.

Threat No. 2. Man is a comfort seeker. Writers have often warned that the sturdy, independent American is fast becoming an "other-directed" personality or an "organization man." This tendency, however recent it may be, has older roots. They go back to the development in the eighteenth and nineteenth centuries of a common-sense ethic, sometimes called bourgeois morality. It followed mathematical rationalism and had more direct effect upon everyday life. After all, only a few people are mathematicians, but everyone claims common sense.

This ethic guides the respectable citizen, who is in business for a profit, who keeps his bargains, pays his debts, rarely kicks up a commotion. Such virtues usually pay. Their social value becomes painfully evident whenever people disregard them. But the ethic has little to do with the passionate loyalty and daring courage of an Old Testament prophet or of Jesus.

Some of our forefathers tried hard to show that this new ethic was Christian. Others were rather proud that it was *not* the Christian ethic. They boasted of their skepticism and radical independence of authority. Some of them struck bold blows for freedom, but more of them were merely stuffy.

It takes conviction to *do* anything remarkable. The skeptics, lacking strong convictions, often became conformists.

Thus, though this bourgeois ethic cleared away some old-fashioned hokum, it introduced some new hokum of its own. Jeremy Bentham's "utilitarian" ethic taught the sensible man how to get the most pleasure in the long run with the least painful consequences. It even offered a "calculus of pleasure"—a formula to guide behavior. Bentham *almost* perfected his theory to the point where the calculating machine could figure morality better than a man. Decision, guilt, and sacrifice were obsolete. Once again man was losing his selfhood.

Threat No. 3. Man is a gadget on the assembly line. The industrial revolution of the nineteenth century brought this threat. With this revolution came vast factories, the modern metropolis, the modern suburb, the modern war. All of us enjoy its benefits and breathe its spirit. We also carry its burden.

One example shows the point. A new phrase entered the language: "the labor market." If we were not so used to it, we might think it one of the most gruesome phrases ever invented. A person's labor—a self in action—is a commodity for sale. A factory employs thousands of "hands." Newspaper writers comment dispassionately that the economy works best when there are three or four million unemployed, forming a "labor pool" and permitting flexibility in industry. We easily forget that the hands working or unemployed are persons longing to be human and to plan their own futures.

The standard of living, the relative safety from hunger and disease, the leisure are all gains. But the system which offers these opportunities to selfhood brings perils which have destroyed selves.

Threat No. 4. Man is an animal. Darwin published his *Origin of Species* in 1859. The hypothesis of organic evolution, supported by a mass of data, cleared up a lot of chaotic thought. But the dogma of popular Darwinism, that evolution offered the decisive clue to the nature of man, produced more confusion than clarity. A few enthusiasts worked out a "Social Darwinism," the notion that struggle for survival shows the best way to organize a society. That led to the glorifying of conduct that would normally be considered subhuman.

A Gilbert and Sullivan opera commented:

Darwinian man, though well-behaved,

At best is only a monkey shaved!

Not everyone took that as a joke. The oftener people believed it, the oftener it came true.

There were more threats. But these are enough to mention. Not all drove in the same direction. Any one person will find it hard to believe that he is simultaneously a thinking mechanism, a stodgy conformist, a cog in the industrial process, and a predatory animal. But all the threats, battering at mankind, beat down the self-consciousness of free, responsible persons, capable of decision, of guilt, of heroism.

Yet man resists being caged—even for his own good. When pressures cramp the existential posture, he rebels.

Beginnings of Rebellion

Rebellions seldom stay within channels. This one exploded in many directions. But all its blasts defied a society that nagged or cajoled men to be less than men.

A group of powerful characters asserted the meaning of selfhood in the unique individuality of every person. They appealed to experience—not just the experience that comes through the sense organs but the experience of the total man. They probed the inner depths of the person. They were willing to reason about experience but not to deny it, not to force it into unreal rational patterns. They approached life as actors, not as spectators. They acknowledged a mystery of selfhood that no reasoning could figure out, no industrialism control.

The rebellion came like an earthquake with its preliminary tremors, its massive shocks, its continuing reverberations. The whole action was, and is, intricate. I shall point to just a few major episodes.

The preliminary tremor finds its best symbol in

Pascal (1623-1662). Two centuries ahead of time, his sensitive spirit felt the threats that others would discern much later.

A scientific genius, Pascal pushed forward the frontiers of physics and mathematics. He was thrilled with the power of the mind, which makes tiny man greater than the colossal universe which cannot think. Like Descartes, he declared that man without thought simply would not be man.

But then he rebelled against the whole rationalistic spirit of his age. Inventing a calculating machine, he showed that in its ability to solve problems it was more like man than any animal, but that it lacked life. And he asked the haunting question: What does it mean to be a living person in this universe that science is discovering? He looked for the meaning *for persons* of a cosmos that runs so blindly, so mathematically, not even knowing that people are here. He wrote: "The eternal silence of these infinite spaces frightens me." And he wondered: "Who has put me here? By whose order and direction have this place and time been allotted to me?"[2]

Although he was both scientist and Christian, Pascal was totally uninterested in the popular attempts to show that nature proves there is a God. The issue, he said, is not to know something *about* deity, but to love and trust a merciful God. We find God, not by *objective calculations* but by *personal decision* of venturing trust. The lostness of man in the infinite spaces, the wretchedness of the sinner without God are the experiences that lead man to God. So this master of scientific reasoning declared, "The heart has its reasons, which reason does not know."[3]

As a Roman Catholic in controversy with the Pope, Pascal worried about the sources of authority. Although he often appealed to the Bible and Christian tradition, he found his own "call" to speak in no external authority, but simply in "the necessity of speaking."[4]

In many ways Pascal was an existentialist before his time: in his appeal to personal experience, his shift from objectivity to involvement, his exploration of anxiety and guilt, his acceptance of responsibility for urgent individual decision. But people were not ready to listen. The time was coming when they would be.

Existentialism Arrives

Society and philosophy pushed the lid down on rebellions like Pascal's. But as the lid pressed tighter, the pressures underneath got more intense. By the nineteenth century they let go. The Victorian century, the time that appears confident, complacent, and rather boring, was the time of the protesting giants who managed to shake the foundations of their age and ours.

Sören Kierkegaard (1813-1855) made existentialism a self-conscious movement and created much of its vocabulary. From his lookout in Denmark he saw a European society smothering itself in conformity and rationalism. He set out to jab it and irritate it. He ridiculed the philosophers (like Hegel) whose grandiose systems *answered* all the questions—without even *asking* the main question: *Who am I? What does it mean to be an existing person? What insecurities and inner agonies are covered over by these foolishly confident explanations of all reality?* I shall look further at his major themes in the next chapter.

Halfway across the continent the troubled Russian, Fyodor Dostoevsky (1821-1881), poured out his anxieties and his thirst for freedom in mighty novels. Especially in his *Notes from Underground* [5] he depicted a troubled character, both repulsive and fascinating, who made a prophetic complaint. He derided irreverently any "laws of nature" which, with stone-wall stubbornness, denied that he was free, calculated with cause-effect certainty whether or not he could make a face at someone, and turned him from a man into a "piano-key." He decided that if he did not like "twice two makes four," he would not be reconciled to it. Likewise he attacked the bourgeois morality of prosperity and peace, a morality which assumed that man lives "to keep out of the rain." He preferred to act out of spite or caprice or stupidity, to seek suffering and fantastic dreams, in order to achieve what is "most precious" of all: individuality.

Back in Germany, Friedrich Nietzsche (1844-1900) made passionate outbursts against the cult of mediocrity and conformity. Nietzsche has had a bad press—which, no doubt, he asked for—but his message has gone on to trouble the world. He ridiculed the timid morality of the churches and announced that God is dead. Yet the famous psychologist C. G. Jung has said that "history cannot support many men as religious as Nietzsche."[6] Every person, exulted Nietzsche, is a "unique wonder," never to be repeated in all history. But men, liking comfort and inertia, afraid of their neighbors, yield to their herd-instinct and reject "the greatest joy of existence"—to "live dangerously." Nietzsche's writings pulse with the sense of striving and of despair.

Completely opposed to these men in many ways was the man nobody could ignore, Karl Marx (1818-1883). But he was at least halfway an existentialist. Rejecting the spectator-role, Marx declared that whereas other philosophers tried to describe reality, he proposed to change it. He fought the industrial system which stifled personal freedom and "alienated" men from each other and from the products of their work. It is ironical that the Marxist philosophy, which aimed to free men, has enslaved so many. The blame rests partly on Marx, the prisoner of his own dogmatism, and partly on those who have used his name in their own cruel drive to subject men.

These intense, dramatic men (Pascal, Kierkegaard, Dostoevsky, Nietzsche, and Marx), with little or no co-operation among themselves, have managed to shift the terms on which men live today. All of them were abnormal characters. All had bad health. They were lonely, having no friends or treating their friends badly. All were sufferers. Three skirted insanity. Not one was the type a mother hopes her boy will turn out to be.

Then why not reject and ignore them? Well, anyone will reject much that they did. But ignoring them is harder. Their sickness foreshadowed the deep sickness of society that has destroyed so many lives in the twentieth century. They help us to understand ourselves. And they point, in perverse or in admirable ways, to the fact that persons can become more than "well-adjusted" fragments of the social mass.

One more man, who was not an existentialist but who belongs in this story, is Sigmund Freud (1856-1939). Some existentialists aim a sharp attack on Freud for tracing human decisions to hidden compulsions rather than to freedom. But by clinical methods this physician confirmed part of what the existentialists had been saying in poetic and dramatic language. However Freud's specific conclusions may be modified, his recognition of a self below the surface is here to stay. After Freud it is hard to imagine that anyone will ever again say, "I am a thing that thinks."

The nineteenth-century existentialists did not convince everyone. Many people did not even hear about them. More pretended that they did not. But the age-old existential posture had become an "ism."

Perhaps it should not be called an "ism." Its furious energy breaks through all formulas, and most of its spokesmen resent being "typed" by a name. But convenience needs a vocabulary. So in this book *existentialism* is the diverse movement coming out of the modern revolt. As for adjectives, *existential* refers to the perennial posture; *existentialist* to the modern movement and its distinctively modern posture.

Whatever we call it, the revolt had a future. It was destined for a new burst of energy in Europe after the First World War, in all the Western World after the Second.

FOUR
THE DISTURBING DANE

"THAT INDIVIDUAL" IS THE EPITAPH Sören Kierkegaard proposed for himself. And "that individual" he was.

In a double sense he is the central figure in existentialism. First, he set the style of the movement in writings unforgettably fervent, glittering, tempestuous, witty, and devout. Second, he was the living existentialist, involved to the hilt in all that he wrote. Like ancient Socrates, who *talked* and *was* philosophy, Kierkegaard both *wrote* and *lived* existentialism.

It is tempting to examine his life. The materials are dramatic enough: his lonely oddity of appearance and character; his burden of his father's guilt and his own; his courtship and engagement to Regina; his agonizing break with her, due partly to inner conflicts, partly to a peculiar sense of vocation; his double life as a public "frivolous bird" and a private "penitent"; his prolific writings in a short career; his inner torment and experience of grace; his attack upon the church in the name of faithfulness to Christ.

Furthermore, on Kierkegaard's own advice we should look at him. In true existentialist manner he derides the practice of separating the writing from the writer. He invites us to look at himself —so that he may make us look at ourselves. His own life he called "an epigram calculated to make people aware." Richard Niebuhr describes him in a vivid sentence. He shows us a "series of signs on the road, which read 'This way to the signpost' "; then "when we arrive at the signpost we will find a hand pointing nowhere except directly at us."[1]

But this is a very short book. So, with a profound apology to Kierkegaard, I shall say little more of his career and get on to his writings. After a slow start—a Danish writer reaches few people at first—his works have come to reverberate through Europe and America. Unavailable in English until 1936 (eighty-one years after Kierkegaard's death), his books now fill long shelves in scholarly libraries and dot the stands of the wildest paperback book stores. The disturbing Dane has found his audience.

It would be *absurd* (to use one of his favorite words) to sum up Kierkegaard's teachings. He does not lay out his ideas in orderly fashion. Anyone who puts them in order distorts them. Like a literary boxer, Kierkegaard jabs, feints, catches his reader off-balance. He drives you (for his writings are always directed at *you)* into a corner, pummels you, offers you a way out and dares you to take it. He makes you laugh as he turns his whiplike wit on someone, then agonize as the backlash catches you. He pours out sarcasms and invective, then instantaneously shifts to humble and reverent prayer.

Yet I shall try the risky business of describing a few of the themes that he infused into existentialism.

The Critique of Rationalism

Everyone who dislikes the existentialists calls them *irrationalists.* That seems to end discussion. Actually, however, it only raises an issue.

Diderot, the French revolutionist, once wrote satirically: "Astray at night in an immense forest, I have only a small light to guide me. A stranger comes along and tells me: 'My friend, blow out your candle so as to see your way better.' This stranger is a theologian."[2]

That is a devastating blow—if it connects. Perhaps it is a wild haymaker that misses most theologians (who, after all, make a career of *reasoning* about religion). But all the heirs of Diderot think that his punch hits squarely the existentialists. The existentialist has an answer. He says that Diderot's man in the woods can make a fool of himself in two ways. (1) He can blow out the light. (2) He can assume that his candle is a giant searchlight which illumines the whole woods and takes all the risk out of his adventure.

If error No. 1 is stupidity, error No. 2 is a crazed hallucination. The wise man will use all the light he has, without deceiving himself about how much he has. Pascal, years before Diderot, said that there is "nothing so conformable to reason" as a certain "disavowal of reason."[3]

All the existentialists try to determine, as accurately as possible, the extent of reason's light. All reason as much as they can. But all refuse to deny experiences that they cannot explain (as I refuse to deny gravitation even though I cannot explain it). And, going further, they insist that reason can never remove from life the risk of personal decision.

Kierkegaard understands very well that objective reasoning about evidence is the only way to settle some questions. He knows that people trap themselves in their illusions, that detachment from factual reality is insanity. But, he continues, it is not enough that a man know the objective truth; he must himself be truthfully related to the objective reality. Kierkegaard makes the point with one of his characteristic stories.[4]

A man escapes from an insane asylum. He decides to convince people that he is sane by talking rationally. Finding a ball on the ground, he puts it in the tail pocket of his coat. As he walks, the ball bounces against his rear end. And at every bounce, he says, "Bang, the earth is round." Though he tells *the objective truth,* he does not demonstrate his sanity. Now, says Kierkegaard, he would not do better to say that the earth is flat. Objective truth is better than objective falsity. But more important than both is *subjective truth* —that is, the truth of *a subject* (a person) rightly related to reality. That is the meaning of the repeated statements: "Truth is subjectivity."[5] "Truth consists precisely in inwardness."[6]

Consequently, says Kierkegaard, man can be related to God only "by virtue of the infinite passion of inwardness."[7] The attempts to get at God by objective logical arguments are ridiculous. Although Kierkegaard sees the flaws which logicians have found in the "proofs" of God's existence, his major objection is something else. To stand apart from God and try to prove his reality is to remove oneself from the inward relation which alone makes possible any knowledge of God. With typically flamboyant rhetoric he says: "So rather let us sin, sin out and out, seduce maidens, murder men, commit highway robbery. . ."[8] God can still get at us. But when we coolly stand off from God and try to prove that he is there, he cannot reach us.

Rationalism, whether in theology or in general philosophy, has never quite recovered its old health since the battering of the pioneer existentialist. But Kierkegaard's attack, taken on its own terms, involves two major problems. He is shrewd enough to know this, but he prefers to leave the problems with people rather than offer a premature solution.

1. Like all Christians since the Apostle Paul, Kierkegaard sees the "offense" and the "foolishness" to our normal inclinations in the gospel of God's act in Christ. Then he goes on to exult so much in the "absurdity" of faith that anybody impressed by him must wonder whether reason can do anything at all to distinguish truth from nonsense in religion. Kierkegaard believes that there is a distinction and that it is made primarily by personal integrity rather than by logical analysis. Even so, he is adept at using all the tools of logic to expose nonsensical errors in sentimental

or hypocritical religion. Clearly he does not abandon all rationality in his attacks on rationalism.

2. Sometimes Kierkegaard suggests that it does not greatly matter what a person believes so long as he believes it with whole-hearted commitment. He compares the pagan idolater, praying "with the entire passion of the infinite," and the conventional Christian, praying "in a false spirit." There is not much doubt that he prefers the pagan and persuades his reader to do the same.[9] But he later goes on to attack a "devilish" wisdom which proclaims that it makes no difference what a man wills so long as that is what he wills. It is almost as though he foresees what some Nietzscheans and Sartreans will later do or what some Americans will justify under the slogan of "doing your own thing." His answer is that it matters that man will the good.[10] In his total thought Kierkegaard skillfully plays these two themes against each other, leaving the tension unresolved. To this day it haunts existentialism. Some extentialists put great store in the *content* of belief; others think the *passion* of commitment is the truly important thing. Yet all despise formal belief without commitment, and all find some beliefs abhorrent.

Self-Discovery

Existentialism, we have noticed, starts with the question: "Who am I? What does it mean for me to exist as a unique individual?" That turns out to be an impossibly difficult question. No one ever answers it. But to begin to answer it, even to ask it in all seriousness, is a momentous event.

The great obstacle to an answer is that each of us fears to understand himself. Living by false self-images, we lack the nerve to explore ourselves without illusion. Personality is fiendishly elusive in its tricks of self-deception.

If we begin to get past the delusions we discover at the core of selfhood a deep *anxiety.* (In everyday language the word *anxiety* has become so trivial that existentialists often use the German *Angst,* which sounds more profound. Or they translate Kierkegaard's Danish into *dread.*) Some people will not admit their own anxiety or may not even recognize it. They are the cowards who manage to cover up. Those with the honesty to see themselves can discover this anxiety. Almost everybody has moments of insight when he catches this truth.

What causes such anxiety? The plainest answer is simply that *life is insecure.* And man can see beyond his own limitations just enough to crave the security he never attains. He finds tentative security in home or job or reputation. But, unless he is an expert in self-deception, he knows that these are all temporary, as he is himself temporary. Absolutely nothing in this world can satisfy his craving.

Furthermcre, man has the dizzying privilege of choosing what he will be. Of course, heredity and environment enter in. But each of us does something with his heredity and environment. *Our decisions make ourselves.* Once in all time exists this specific self, able to do and be what no one else can do and be. This is the anxious, the "dreadful" responsibility of each self.

At this point many people ask: Is all this necessary: What good can such talk do? Of course, there is a lot of anxiety around. But doesn't talking, about it simply ruin people's confidence? Isn't it more healthy to forget it and be moderately happy without such worries?

The existentialist answer, contrary to some rumors, is not a sour desire to see everybody turn morose. Existentialists can enjoy parties, friendship, sports. (Kierkegaard was a devotee of the theater.) But, says the existentialist, when you enjoy life, know what you are doing.

Yes, many people get along fairly well in a mediocre, conventional sort of life. As long as health and finances are favorable, the neighbors decent, the children out of trouble, and the nation out of war, they feel pretty secure.

But this security is an evasion. It is always vulnerable. A change of events (cancer, war, bad luck) can bring the roof crashing in at any moment, for life is basically insecure. Furthermore, this mediocrity settles for a sub-human level of living instead of genuine existence. It saves one from the awful anxiety of taking responsibility for the making of a self.

If Kierkegaard is right, our churches actually harm us when they develop cults of "peace of mind" and "positive thinking." They encourage evasion instead of honest self-searching. They would do better to tear away our illusions, until we see ourselves in our "sickness unto death." Only then will healing really be possible.

Kierkegaard tries to work past our normal tricks of deception in his famous description of the three stages of life. In the *aesthetic stage,* where we all have a yen to live, one takes life in terms of unfettered enjoyment. Like a stone skipping on the surface of the water, he gaily tastes the delights of life. But as the stone must sink, the aesthetic life must end in despair. Enjoyment without commitment cannot support it for long.

Despair then drives one to decision. In resolute choice one becomes a real person. Struggle and responsibility are the marks of real selfhood. But this *ethical stage* brings experiences of remorse and penitence. It is no use to say, with perhaps a sidelong glance at the Kinsey report, that one's behavior is as good as average, for ethical decision means commitment, and human beings are half-hearted in their commitments. Once again the result is despair.

Now the self must either revive the futile hopes that have already failed it—or drive on to the *religious stage.* Here a person knows himself as an individual responsible to God. He learns the meaning of sin and suffering, with all the cheap veils torn away. For sin is not just a nasty act. It is the fear and distrust that keep us away from God. But to know oneself as a suffering sinner is a gain. Suffering has a grandeur that was missing in the falsity of a life that kept trying not to suffer. And suffering may open the way to the knowledge of God's love, which brings joy and peace rather than despair. The aesthetic and ethical, not destroyed but dethroned, will then find their rightful place in true existence. But that outcome depends upon "the leap of faith."

The Leap of Faith

The only answer to radical despair is radical trust. But we prefer not to be so radical. We like to move gradually into faith, without ever letting go of the old efforts at security. We aim to make the gap so easy that someone can cross it without ever realizing it. We are, says Kierkegaard, like a comic character in a Danish play, who "little by little, reached the point of assuming that almost having passed his examinations was the same as having passed them."[12] Or we are like the poor swimmer who wants to keep a toe on the bottom rather than trust himself to the water. He is not really a swimmer until he "ventures far out," abandoning the support of the bottom for the support of the water. Faith is like lying on "70,000 fathoms of water," relying solely on the buoyancy of the sea.

It is important to notice that Kierkegaard is not describing the psychology of instantaneous conversion. A person usually struggles through a long period of time, just as he may very gradually learn to swim. Still there is the decisive difference between trusting the waves and trusting a foot-hold on the bottom. What Kierkegaard is saying is that there can be no Christianity without venturing, without dangerous trust in God. "Without risk there is no faith."

Hence faith requires a "leap." This leap is not, as is sometimes said, a kind of desperate lurch of the emotions that leaves the mind behind. It is a decision of the *whole* self—mind, will, feeling. But no one coasts into faith.

The real problem is not (as we like to think) doubt versus faith. If so, there might be any number of halfway points. One could move from doubt to probability to virtual certainty. But the actual conflict is despair and defiance versus trust. Here there are no halfway points.

Thus Kierkegaard upsets a great deal of conventional talk about Christianity. The important question is *not* "What are the Christian beliefs?" In fact, that question is often a cowardly escape from the real question: "How can I become a Christian?"

And to become a Christian, says Kierkegaard, is to become *contemporaneous* with Christ. So long as Christ is somebody, even a very important somebody, who lived many centuries ago, I have less to do with him than with many people whom I meet nowadays. If he becomes my contemporary, then I know his commands and promises are addressed *to me*. The Christian shares in the suffering and courage of Christ.

Yet Christ is an *offense* to mankind. His com-

mands are cruelly severe. Even his kindliest statements are offensive. "Come hither, all ye that la-
bour and are heavy laden, I will give you rest."[13]
That sounds very lovely and peaceful. But look
who says it! The humblest of men. Someone who,
unlike the foxes and birds, has no place to lay his
head. Someone who leads us to Golgotha. How can
such a person be the God-man? No wonder we
cannot by common sense ease our way into faith.
No wonder faith is a daring leap.

And it is a continuous leap. No one can say with
satisfaction, "Last year I made the leap. Now I
have landed on the other side. Now I have faith."
Even if in some crisis I conquered my fears, the
next threat may find me vulnerable again. So
faith is both a constant, and a risky venture. So
one lives in "fear and trembling." For "fear and
trembling signifies that a God exists."[14]

The Attack upon Christendom

It takes no great brains to see that people prefer
to avoid this kind of leap. Yet they would find it
embarrassing to come out openly and reject Christian faith. So society and the churches have invented a new technique to spare mankind.
Gradually they have transformed Christianity to
mean the very opposite of the New Testament.
They have made Christianity stand for the conventional, comfortable life that everybody desires,
instead of for lonely, courageous obedience to
Christ.

Worship has become hypocrisy. A comfortable preacher talks to a comfortable congregation about the glory of sacrifice and humility—and, says Kierkegaard, nobody laughs. The more eloquently the preacher describes the sufferings of Christ, the more successful, prosperous, and comfortable the preacher becomes.

Thus we conspire to "make a fool" out of God. And it turns out to be easy to do—easier than making a fool out of some stupid person; for God, who in his unchangeable majesty might be invulnerable to us, lets us hurt him—as he showed on Golgotha. And he lets us make a fool out of him.

But, says Kierkegaard, "I would rather gamble, carouse, fornicate, steal, murder, than take part in making a fool of God."[15] Our dishonest worship and our easy assumption that we are Christians turn out to be our worst sins.

The passionate question which comes to dominate Kierkegaard's writings is *How can one become a Christian in Christendom?* "Christendom has done away with Christianity, without being quite aware of it."[16] If we knew nothing of Christ, the message about him might shock us into a decision of loyalty or rejection. But now we are immune. Thinking that we already are Christians, we are undisturbed.

In the last months of his life, Kierkegaard set out to deliver the needed shock. In a series of newspaper articles and pamphlets he attacked the sham of the established religion. His weapons range from the tiny rapier to heavy artillery. The reader both delights in his skill in combat and feels the pain of getting wounded.

Sometimes Kierkegaard's attack is extremely bitter. He comes close to the heresy of saying that the world is evil. He almost forgets, it seems, that Gospel means "Good News."

But he does know how to tell the Gospel. As he wrote in his journal, "This is all I have known for certain, that God is love. Even if I have been mistaken on this or that point: God is nevertheless love."[17]

FIVE
THE FRACTURED FAMILY

THE LONELY BACHELOR, Sören Kierkegaard, left no biological offspring. But his intellectual and spiritual heirs are a large and noisy tribe. They can never possibly hold a family reunion. Not only are they scattered too far. Even if they could be collected, the occasion would make the wildest dog fight look mild. But let an innocent rationalist of the pre-existentialist variety—there are a few left—walk into their midst, and they forget their internal feuds to gang up on him.

Not all these existentialists claim descent from Kierkegaard. Nor do I mean to imply he is the main impulse behind the whole group. Some owe more to Nietzsche or Luther or Dostoevsky or even to Marx. But somewhere in the family tree of all is "that individual." Or, at the very least, he has shaken the limbs of all the family trees.

The Great Divide

It is natural that existentialism should fragment into bewildering variety. It sees all the irrationalities in life and fights its way through them by acts of will. It announces that the important truth is not the objective facts on which we can all agree, but the personal truth which the self confesses. Hence every act of self-discovery by a struggling individual brings something new into the history of existentialism.

Running through the many divisions is one

which works like a continental divide. Some existentialists, living on opposite sides of the divide, can scarcely see or talk across it. Others, living nearer, shout across it daily. And a few perch precariously on the divide itself, equally inclined to slip off on either side. Yet all know the divide is there, affecting them at every moment. On the one side are those whose lives are a passionate cry for God. On the other side are the clamorous atheists.

Why, people often wonder, can such contrary voices sound from the same movement? We can best see why if we think of Kierkegaard's "leap of faith." In self-discovery, with its revelation of insecurity, despair, and guilt, comes the moment when one sees the futility of many human concerns. Only then can he make the leap.

For the men of faith this leap is the highest act of courage. It means the shaking off of all illusions, the daring venture to truth. He who leaps must leave behind the many who cling to their insecurities. They are too timid to let go. Bound to convention, dependent on their illusions, they must keep at least one toe on the beach, even through the waves may at any moment wash away this footing. They can never know the glorious freedom of answering God's call —of casting off onto 70,000 fathoms of water.

The atheists accept the first part of this description. They agree in the courageous unmasking of illusions. But, they say, the men of faith refuse to follow the adventure to the end. Their leap of faith is itself one more illusion. Actually beyond the leap is *nothing*. Courage acknowledges the nothing and says openly that the only resources of the self are within the self. Without weeping or wailing, we had better recognize that life is a trap. No one can rescue us from the trap. The only victory is defiance and the assertion of freedom.

Both these groups are trying to be utterly honest. That is, they are trying to be as nearly honest as human beings can become, because all existentialists know that in the devious ways of self-deception no one is completely honest. Why do two groups, both reporting the reality they see, bring such different reports? Because the *will* has as much as the mind to do with anyone's account of life. So the issue really is one of courage—not of bravado or of seeing who can shout loudest, "See how bold I am," but of steadfast courage.

That is why existentialism has produced some of the most penetrating testimonies of faith and some of the most ruthless declarations of atheism in our time. As Carl Michalson has aptly said, existentialism is at the least a road to Golgotha. "But at the end of that road one may as easily find . . only two thieves as find the suffering savior."[1]

The "Death of God"

The trumpet call of the atheistic existentialists sounded from Nietzsche in 1882. "God is dead". The proof? Look at the churches. They are the tombs of God. Their timidity and complacent mediocrity are the overwhelming evidence that no God reigns over them or calls men to dangerous faith.

Notice how close Nietzsche's atheism comes to Kierkegaard's Christianity. Kierkegaard had accused the churches of making a fool of God. Nietzsche, knowing nothing of Kierkegaard's protest, declares that the churches are God's sepulchers. So close and so vastly distant are the Christian and the atheist.

God is dead, says Nietzsche, because we human beings have killed him. This mighty deed is reason both to exult and to tremble. We have murdered the holy and powerful deity! No greater act can there be. No ordinary rite of atonement can cleanse us. What then can we do? "Shall we not ourselves have to become gods, merely to seem worthy of it?"[2]

All this is either adolescent bravura or a piercing declaration of human responsibility. The existentialists constantly argue which it is. In either case it is a powerful irritant to the religiosity of a society which assumes that the building of churches is an evidence of faith. It may be that people give their millions of dollars to churches each year because they want to bury God.

More than three-quarters of a century after Nietzsche's declaration, his words found a pale echo in a "death-of-God theology" thats made a flurry in the mid-1960's. To the press the idea of the death of God seemed new and spectacular;

THE FRACTURED FAMILY 61

actually what was new in it was that *theologians* —not philosopher-poets like Nietzsche—should say that God is dead. Theology, most people assumed and the derivation of the word implied, is about God. But these theologians were seriously aiming to be Christian. They shifted the center of faith from God to Jesus Christ.

A contradictory set of impulses was at work in this theology. One impulse, coming out of a skeptical impulse akin to logical positivism, said that man simply has no basis for his metaphysical speculations. Christians had better quit talking about God (and all that the word implies for a theory of the universe including its beginnings and endings) and talk about Jesus, whom they know something about and who makes a claim on them. The contradictory impulse established a grandiose metaphysics, saying that God really had lived for many aeons but had at length died —sometimes it was said on the cross at Golgotha, sometimes in the 19th or 20th century—as an act of sacrifice to give freedom and responsibility to man. . .[3]

Partly because of these differences the death-of-God theologians never formed a movement and their vogue was brief. Another reason for the quick cresting of the idea was that its spokesmen —quite contrary to Nietzsche, who despised the masses—made great use of mass communications; and the press gives and takes away fame swiftly.

But existentialist atheism has a longer history. It made its way more slowly, and it will not fade away quickly. What it has to say is immensely important.

Twentieth-Century Atheism

In this century the atheists have been the loudest of the existentialists. Where the movement has become a fad, its mood has often been "God-be-damned" or "God-be-forgotten"—if those phrases can be taken not as casual profanity but in their most literal meaning. Even when atheism has been most blatant and irreverent, it has often come close to profound seriousness. We can readily see this even in a hasty look at three major writers. In the next few pages, I shall, at the cost of ignoring many things they say, point toward their significance for the one question of faith in God.

Jean-Paul Sartre (b. 1905) is the man who made existentialism famous. Successively a teacher and novelist, soldier, prisoner of war who escaped, worker on an underground newspaper of the French Resistance Movement during the Nazi occupation, he came into his greatest prominence when the war ended. His novels, short stories, and plays reached an audience that never reads technical philosophy. Living an off-beat life in Paris, he was the picturesque person about whom a coterie could readily gather. The nonconformists (who usually like to rebel within some cultic conformity) found him their man. Americans in Paris stopped to gape at Sartre, writing in his favorite barroom, and brought back a legend that made it hard to take the man seriously. What they overlooked was (1) a French tradition of writing in cafés and (2) Sartre's unheated hotel room which made it rather practical for him to write in the near-by bar.

Actually Sartre was, even then, a serious philosopher and man of letters, and in the years since then he has earned unquestioned eminence. His atheism, although it began early and suddenly, is the outcome of a long pilgrimage. As he describes it, it began one day when he was twelve years old, waiting for some late schoolmates. "After a while, not knowing what else to do to occupy my mind, I decided to think of the Almighty. Immediately He tumbled into the blue and disappeared without giving any explanation. He doesn't exist, I said to myself with polite surprise, and I thought the matter was settled."[4]

But, says Sartre long after, he continued to believe—in a sense—in "the Invisible One, the Holy Ghost." What he means is that he continued to believe that he had an almost divine destiny. Undoubtedly he realizes with irony that he was often called "the High Priest of existentialism." In retrospect he says that even in the period of some of his most famous atheistic writings he believed that he was somehow "elect," that he had a guarantee of his security.

At last, Sartre believes, he has seen through his illusions, has thrown out the Holy Ghost. To believers and atheists alike he warns: "atheism is a cruel and long-range affair; I think I've carried it through."[5]

In this atheism Sartre is less concerned to disprove God than to insist that God's existence, even if it were true, would make no difference. In one of his earlier statements that I think he would still stand by (even though it comes from the period of "the Holy Ghost"), he wrote: "What man needs is to find himself again and to understand that nothing can save him from himself, not even a valid proof of the existence of God."[6]

That last sentence calls for examination. Suppose Kierkegaard could read it. In one sense, he would say, Sartre could not be more right. A proof of God's existence can save no one. All the objective props for security are futile. Man does need to discover himself. But then, the Danish pioneer would continue, man will never discover himself until he understands his own brief and troubled time against the background of the eternal reality which gave him life. And he will respond to eternity either in rebellion or in trust.

But Sartre has an answer. His atheism, for better or for worse, has a positive purpose. He wants man to take responsibility for himself, to make his own decisions—yes, to create his own values. For this reason he refused the 1964 Nobel Prize for Literature rather than acknowledge the authority of a prestigious institution. For the same reason he cannot acknowledge the authority of church or God. Religion is too ready to buck responsibilities onto God. The religious man, instead of making his decision and taking the consequences, is likely to run to God to find out what to do.

That argument may hurt. It may remind the Protestant Christian of a similar dart that he has thrown at the Roman Catholic. Have not Protestants scorned the authoritarianism of Rome and the dependence of the Roman Catholic who can find an answer to every moral dilemma by asking his priest? (The priest, it is assumed, either has been taught the answer or can look it up in a book on casuistry.) Has Sartre driven the Protestant position to its logical conclusion—or absurdity— in a sort of priesthood of all unbelievers?

Perhaps so. But not necessarily. Once again the question is whether the "leap of faith" is a courageous response to the God who truly is or a flight into illusion. The Protestant Christian can at least answer Sartre that *responsibility*—that favorite existentialist word—gets its meaning from *response*. The Christian lives by response to the Holy God who is his Creator. He testifies that in those moments (however rare) when he responds in grateful trust, he answers a call to more daring adventure and more genuine freedom than in the moments (however often) when he defies God.

Albert Camus (1913-1960) for a while stood close to Sartre, both in personal friendship and in public impact, but then the two men took different directions at the cost of some personal estrangement. The resemblance was closest at the time when Camus was writing *The Myth of Sisyphus* and *The Stranger*, two short books that form a pair.

In *The Myth of Sisyphus* Camus makes a parable of the life of man out of the ancient Greek story of the hero condemned by the gods to push a boulder up a hill throughout eternity, with the realization that whenever he neared the top of the hill, the boulder would roll back down and he would have to start over. Human life, like the situation of Sisyphus, is absurd. By using the word absurd, Camus does not mean to say that we cannot reason about life and trace some rational connections between cause and effect. He uses the word to point out the contrast, as he sees and feels it, between the aspirations of man and the silence of the universe. Between man and the rest of nature there is "opposition, laceration, and divorce." Yet Sisyphus, symbol of existentialist man, attains a kind of happiness through the sheer assertion of courage in the face of the hostile gods.

The Stranger puts the same theme into fiction. You can read it in an hour or so, but you may then want to take a day to re-read it. Its hero, or anti-hero, is a stranger to his mother, his fiancée, his business associates—and a stranger to any consistent motivation or sense of meaning. In the absurdity of his existence he kills an Algerian Arab without knowing why, and he is sentenced to death, less because of the murder than because he did not grieve over his mother's death, as the jury thought he should. Only when he has come to terms with the certainty of death does he achieve a kind of resolution and happiness in the face of "the benign indifference of the universe."

There is a remarkable similarity between *The Stranger* and Sartre's short story, *The Wall*. Both tell of the transformation of a man, condemned to death, from apathetic cowardice to courage. But both tell also the message of absurdity.

Camus, however, could not stay here. He was a man of great compassion, and he became increasingly impressed with the meaning of human community, especially when men share in suffering. He also became troubled by the wrong in inflicting present suffering on men—communism was one example he had in mind—for the sake of some future ideal, and he moved to a near-pacifism. These themes he developed in his novel, *The Plague*. Concurrently he wrote his longest book, *The Rebel,* in which he argued that man does not simply will values into existence, but owes loyalty to values that are given in a common human nature.

Camus renounced the designation of existentialist. I think of him as a "tragic humanist," that is, a man loyal to human values, yet aware of the tragic quality of the quest to realize them. The tragedy is inherent both in the nature of the universe that confronts man and in the nature of man himself. As he explored this latter theme, especially in the fiction of his last years, he kept working on some of the existentialist themes. His collection of short stories, *Exile and the Kingdom,* tells of men always related to, yet always estranged from a "kingdom" of community and meaning. And his short novel, *The Fall,* is probably the most Christ-haunted book ever written by an atheist.

The death of Camus in an auto accident, at the height of his powers, is as powerful an example of the absurd as anything he wrote. We can only wonder what he might be saying if he were living now. Camus was always *en route.*

I come last to Martin Heidegger (b. 1889). Perhaps I should have taken him first, since his career started before those of Sartre and Camus and he influenced them both. But he is the most forbidding of the three to approach, and it is frightening to try to say something about him in a few paragraphs. Maybe, after looking at Sartre and Camus, it will be barely possible.

Heidegger, some years ago, was frequently called an atheist. But he never should have been, and nobody calls him that any more. He does not accept the designation, any more than he accepts the name of theist. Perhaps he lives directly on the continental divide.

He writes in a notoriously difficult language, which some call German and some call Heideggerian. The style is not simply carelessness or German pedantry; Heidegger is trying to evoke something in his reader, not tell him what to think. His first great work, *Being and Time,* analyzed some of the experiences of human existence in profound and intricate detail. Then his writings became increasingly cryptic and evocative. One of them, called *Holzwege* (paths in the woods) suggests by its title that man does not have a map of the universe or his own pilgrimage, but can only sketch out some pathways. Increasingly Heidegger has turned his attention to a few poets, to the uses of language, and to the problem of interpretation.

I might, at the cost of some exaggeration, get at Heidegger by saying that his favorite subject is *nothing.* If this seems to be an unpromising start, it turns out to have interesting possibilities. The most fundamental fact about selfhood, he says, is that each of us is constantly drifting toward *nothing.* We shall die, and the decaying corpse that will be left is not a self. Heidegger offers no hint of a continuing life after death. The destiny of the self is to be nothing.

Life is finitude, temporality. The person has been "thrown into" this world. He is not at home here. He has no root here. Yet he has no place except this.

But right here each person has the opportunity to *achieve authentic existence.* (In American vocabulary we might say: to become a genuine self.) Existence is not offered us on a platter. Timidity lures us to drag out our lives on a subhuman level. But *existence* is a possibility. We can attain it through courage. In this courage we recognize that we are surrounded by nothing. (Not that there are not atoms or electromagnetic fields "out there," but there is *nothing for us.*) We have come from nothing and every moment of life is a movement toward nothing. To know and accept this fact is to achieve a self-understanding that can almost be called salvation.

The alternative is inauthentic existence—to live by illusions, to be irresponsible, to stifle conscience, to get swallowed up in the impersonal mass of industrial society, to refuse to be a self or oneself. In Sartre's development of the Heideggerrian themes, the choice is between good faith and bad faith, between honest commitment and hypocrisy or evasion.

Heidegger has described himself as "waiting for God". The similarity to the title of Samuel Beckett's play, *Waiting for Godot,* is obvious; if you ask Beckett whether there is any relation, he will refuse to tell you. Meanwhile, as Heidegger waits, he writes much about "being"—this mystery which is both the source of our lives and the nothing which swallows us up. This identity or near-identity of "Being" and "nothing" may seem to represent paradox driven to the point of perversity, until we recognize that plainly Being is no thing, and no thing may be more akin to nothing than to something. When Heidegger writes about language as the house of Being and the voice of Being, he comes close to the style of some of the mystics.

Clearly enough, Heidegger does not think of himself as a Christian, but he keeps in conversation with Christians. He does not so much deny the reality of God as deny puny gods. There he has something in common with Christian faith. At the end of one of his books, he says that the nature of thinking is determined by the givenness of Being, and that what is given is a gift.[7] There too he has something in common with faith.

Atheists and Saints

Christians usually give little attention to atheism. They are against itand that is that. But maybe that is not enough.

At least three great Christian philosophers, representing quite different traditions, have recently written with penetrating seriousness about atheism: Nicholas Berdyaev (Eastern Orthodox), Jacques Maritain (Roman Catholic), and Paul Tillich (Protestant). I shall say more about each of these in the next chapter. Now, selecting one of them for convenience, I shall concentrate on Maritain's fascinating essay, "The Meaning of Contemporary Atheism".[8]

Maritain first dismisses those atheists who are flippant or who simply do not want to be bothered by God. Then he looks at those who take their stand in bold rejection of the ordinary habits of respectability. And he comes to *some intriguing comparisons between atheists and saints.*

Most of us, drifting with our society, keep up its typical religious practices. As the social conventions change, we change—and hardly know the difference. The serious atheist has a more daring faith, a "greatness and generosity" which his theories take no account of. He risks disapproval. He sees through the idols that lure most people into devotion.

Only the saint is more clear-sighted. He makes the "total, stable, supremely active refusal to accept things as they are." Trusting God, he rejects *all* idols, even the atheistic idols of nature, society, and self.

Maritain thus destroys a common idea. We often put people on a religious spectrum. At the extreme left is the atheist who believes nothing. Then, moving right, we place groups who successively believe more and more, until at the very right we place the true Christian. But perhaps the rigorous atheist is closer to God than those who believe a little, or even than many who believe a lot.

That agrees with Carl Michalson, whom I have already quoted in this chapter. Existentialism of itself, he says, "does not put. . .Christ on the middle cross, but it will put nothing else there, either." Certainly that is better than cluttering up Golgotha with trivial signs of comfort, which save people from facing Christ.

The atheistic existentialists have something to say to Christians who will listen. Christians can reply with the Gospel. But they had better not reply with any cheapened version of the Gospel.

SIX
DIRECTIONS OF FAITH

THE MANY MEN OF FAITH among the existentialists
follow no party line. They cannot, because existentialism rebels against all party lines. It throws
each person back upon himself, there in the inwardness of personal decision to find his faith.
Any faith taken up because of its popularity is
false faith. It is not the leap to God but the rush
to hide from God in the crowd.

Thus, for all their diversity, the religious existentialists concur in protest against trivial religion or easy refuge in authority. They assault all
forms of peace and security which refuse to face
the portentous facts of recent history and the
trembling anxieties of the human spirit. They call
for self-discovery with the courage and pain which
that venture requires. They seek to understand
what our culture—including its wars, its prosperity, and its technology—is doing to persons.

Religious existentialism is as dazzling as a display of fireworks. The most careful description is
likely to miss the major effect of the display: its
movement. At the cost of ignoring some mighty
themes and many subtle nuances, I shall describe
only a few examples. Because most people who
will read this book are Protestants, Roman Catholics, or Jews (or skeptics who may identify with
the preceding chapter), I shall say something
about these three groups.

But before doing so, I must mention two powerful figures who do not quite belong in these groups, but who have influenced them. The first is Nicholas Berdyaev (1874-1948), the brilliant Russian Orthodox thinker, who had the unusual distinction of arrest and exile by both the Czarist and Soviet governments. Berdyaev voiced again Dostoevsky's passionate cry for freedom and the ancient Eastern Church's yearning that man should become divine. His great theme was the uniqueness and creativity of selves in defiance of all "thingification" of persons. Criticizing both communism and capitalism for their use of persons, he urged a "personalist socialism." Berdyaev's ideas fitted neither Eastern Orthodoxy nor any other orthodoxy. But from his home in Paris for the last twenty-five years of his life he spoke compellingly to Christians everywhere.

Second, I should refer to Karl Jaspers (1883-1969) of Germany and Switzerland, who ranks with Heidegger as one of the two most important "philosophers of existence." Entering philosophy by way of medicine and psychiatry, he emphasized more than any other existentialist the importance of science and reason. Yet he hailed Kierkegaard and Nietzsche as the two geniuses who transformed modern thought. They showed that there can be no important thinking without self-comprehension. Borrowing Kierkegaard's word "shipwreck," Jaspers said that only by passing through anxiety and hopelessness could the philosopher find the way to faith and to truth. He chose a road between Kierkegaard and Nietzsche, "between revealed faith and atheism." His "leap" was the "leap to transcending thinking," which brought him to reverence before "Transcendence" but skepticism of Christianity. Although he owed much to the Bible, he regarded as confining some of the doctrines in it which Christians find liberating.

Catholic Objectivity and Existentialism

Traditional Catholicism had one immediate objection to existentialism. Thomism (the philosophy of St. Thomas Aquinas, which has been declared authoritative by several modern Popes) affirms two ways to find religious truth:

1. Some truths can be known by man's reason, even without faith. For example, any sufficiently intelligent person with adequate knowledge of logic and metaphysics can understand the proofs for the existence of God. This "natural theology" is objectively valid for pagans and Christians, sinners and saints.

2. But reason alone cannot reach all the truths necessary for salvation. God has revealed these further doctrines. The Roman Church is their custodian. The Pope, when he defines doctrine, is infallible. The churchman need never be in doubt about any necessary doctrine. He accepts the authority of the church, which holds and transmits the objective deposit of revelation.

Obviously, then, the Roman church fought against some of the favorite themes of Kierkegaard: that proofs of God's existence are not only fallacious but also blasphemous; that all objective authorities are useless; that man flounders helplessly unless he makes the hazardous venture of self-discovery and the leap of faith.

That might seem to settle matters. And for some Roman Catholics it did so. Many simply rejected existentialism as irrational and nihilistic. Pope Pius XII in 1950 condemned several "fictitious theories," including "existentialism, whether atheistic or simply the type that denies the validity of the reason in the field of metaphysics."[1]

But the matter was not settled. For one thing, many existentialist ideas hark back to St. Augustine. Because such potent "heretics" as Luther and Pascal were (in many ways) Augustinian existentialists, Roman doctrine usually keeps Augustine subdued—but he is too great a saint to silence.

Furthermore, Catholicism knows well that acceptance of authoritative, objective doctrines is not enough. The glory and mystery of God are not wrapped up in the doctrines. And the Christian life means, beyond assent to authority, a living obedience and trust. Hence many Catholics find existentialism meaningful. The first major ventures in appropriating it came from several distinguished laymen.

Thus Christopher Dawson, the famous historian, when he gave the Gifford Lectures on the assigned topic of "natural theology," chose to

redefine his subject. Instead of dealing with the
evidences of God's existence in nature, which is
the traditional meaning of natural theology, he
described the actual religious life of many societies.[2] He did not adopt existentialism as such, but
he started from human existence.

Prior to Pius XII's criticism of existentialism,
Jacques Maritain, had written a book maintain-
ing that Thomas Aquinas was the truest existentialist.[3] The Pope's later statement did not
contradict Maritain directly; the two used the
word with different meanings. But there was a
difference of accent. Maritain was able to praise
Kierkegaard, even while reasserting his Thomist
convictions. I have already mentioned his perceptive understanding of the atheism that he nevertheless rejects.

Gabriel Marcel is closer to the main currents of
existentialism than Maritain. A dramatist, musi-
cian, and philosopher, he was not baptized until
he was nearly forty. Describing his experience of
grace, he reached for language reminiscent of
Kierkegaard— "fathoms deep."

Marcel is concerned with the way in which
"mass society," whether totalitarian or demo-
cratic, crushes personality. In "The Broken
World" (to use the title of one of his plays) we
destroy the reality of selves. Marcel's answer is
not the individualism of many existentialists. He
starts with "we" rather than "I" and he says that
"we" do not know each other except as we live in
the "Mystery of Being."[4] Mystery—unlike a prob-

lem, which is something to be solved—is the nexus of the imaginative life. Personality, love, beauty, death, and Being are mysteries. We live in wonder with them.

The papacy of John XXIII brought into the open the existentialist thrust that had been at work in Catholic theology. Pope John was less interested in doctrinal formalism and abstract authority than in the concerns of people. And Vatican II opened the windows to the intellectual breezes and hurricanes moving in the contemporary world. Some of the French Catholic existentialists, who had been subdued in their conversation and writing under Pius XII, spoke their minds openly.

Karl Rahner, perhaps the greatest of Catholic theologians today, has been deeply influenced by Heidegger. Among the younger theologians William J. Richardson calls for recognition of Heidegger's voice as the voice of a friend of theology. This is not to say that these thinkers (and many others who might be mentioned) are part of a Catholic rush to existentialism. It is to say that Catholic theology today both appropriates and criticizes existentialist motifs with the same freedom that any faith might enjoy in its use of contemporary ideas.

Judaism and I-Thou

Many strains of thought enter into the rich diversity of modern Judaism. Orthodoxy, with its emphasis upon law and cult, frequently finds existentialism too iconoclastic. Reform Judaism often accuses it of irrationalism and pessimism. Yet a powerful Jewish existentialism today is stirring thought and devotion, not only in the synagogue but also in churches and schools outside Judaism. It speaks through such pioneers as Franz Rosenzweig (1886-1929) and Martin Buber (1878-1965) and through such second-generation thinkers as Abraham Heschel and Will Herberg.

Buber is the great patriarchal figure whose shadow stretched, first from Austria and Germany, then (after 1938) from Jerusalem, across the world of religious thought. Profoundly Jewish, yet often critical of organized Judaism, he reached many people through the lure of his person and his writings. His thought had deep roots in the Bible and in Hasidism, that fervent stirring among the Jews of Eastern Europe in the eighteenth century. But he wrestled hard with Kierkegaard, Dostoevsky, and Nietzsche, as well as with the later existentialists.

Approving Kierkegaard, Buber says that "man finds the truth to be true only when he stands its test." The existential thinker "stakes his life in his thinking."[5] With Kierkegaard, Buber emphasizes decision, for "if there were a devil," he says, "it would not be one who decided against God, but one who, in eternity, came to no decision."[6]

But Buber goes on to a drastic criticism of Kierkegaard's lonely individualism. The Dane was right in rescuing the unique self from the anonymous mass. But he was wrong in isolating that self from others, wrong in rejecting marriage, wrong in his harshness toward the world, for the unique self becomes a self only in its human relations.

Buber's famous phrase, *I-Thou,* has by this time become almost a cliché. But some ideas are so rich that they cannot be ruined even by the mumblers of clichés, and this is one of them. "In the beginning," says Buber, "is relation." "All real living is meeting."[7] The most basic human word is *I-Thou.* This word is not made by joining two other words; rather it precedes them. Out of the relation emerge the persons, *I* and *Thou.* They could not be persons were it not for the relation.

But another basic word is *I-It.* There is no avoiding this word: "Without *It* man cannot live. But he who lives with *It* alone is not a man."[8] The trouble is that the pressures of living, especially in a mass society, push us to meet the other as *It* rather than as *Thou.* In doing so, we destroy *him* and destroy *ourselves.* For the *I* of *I-Thou* is human, capable of love and of selfhood. The *I* of *I-It* is less than human.

One *Thou* cannot become *It:* the eternal *Thou,* God. He is the true *Thou* of every life. Living and even theology may try to turn God into *It,* to talk *about* Him, to use Him. If so, we are simply deceived.

Buber's magnificient God-intoxication has in it a deeply mystical strain. Yet it never lets the self become one with deity. For God is "over against" us; he does not absorb our selves but makes us selves.

Yearning people of various faiths have responded to the spell of this man who is both poet and analyst. People sick with the depersonalization of life, yet unhappy with the extreme individualism of many existentialists, find in Buber the sense of selfhood in community. Insistently Jewish though he is, he has won the tributes of such major Protestant thinkers as Emil Brunner, Karl Heim, and Reinhold Niebuhr. Another Jew, Will Herberg, describes him as "closer to radical Protestantism" than some Protestant theologians.[9]

Existential Protestantism

Words play tricks on us. *Protest* today usually means a complaint or objection. But when the word Protestant first came into use in Elizabethan England, *protest* had a very different meaning. *Pro* meant *for* (as in *pro and con*). *Test* was the root of *testify*. To protest meant to testify for, to declare oneself, to take the risk of a witness for the faith.

Protestantism, then, was an existential venture. The Protestant did not simply accept by habit the religious ideas and customs handed down to him. He took the responsibility of declaring his own faith. His Christianity was not an objective set of institutional teachings; it was living, daring trust in God. It asked each person to study the Scriptures, to meet God in Christ, to take his stand in the community of faith. So existential was the Protestant Reformation that to say "existential Protestantism" is almost the same as to say "Protestant Protestantism."

But as time passed, Protestantism often got into a rut. For many people it became a conventional, hand-me-down religion, which required less courage than sports or dating. The many movements which depersonalized man (as we have noticed them in Chapter 3) hit the churches along with the rest of society. Then came the existentialist revolt.

In the stable, confident nineteenth century, most people never noticed existentialism. But the twentieth century, with its disastrous wars and vicious cruelties, jarred all civilization. Unless people were to sleep through the convulsions of history (as a remarkable number are doing), they had to take seriously what the existentialists were talking about.

By this time Christian existentialism has, at the least, restored to Protestantism something of the existential posture so characteristic of the Scriptures and of the Reformation. Sometimes it has also introduced into the church some of the distinctive style and vocabulary of the modern revolt. Thus any examination of Protestantism today will show some marks of existentialism, whether in preaching, church school publications, the topics chosen by college students for religious forums, or the communication of the Christian faith to non-Christians.

For instance, the church is less likely than at some times in the past to address the outsider: "Here are the objective reasons that you should believe in God." It is more likely to say: "This community of faith invites you to share in its venture of trust and commitment." It is less likely to announce: "Here is a higher ethic and better belief than ever before." It is more likely to declare: "Here is a Good News of healing for the anxieties and sicknesses of mankind."

This change has been more clearly stated in theology than anywhere else in the life of the church. Surely the most influential Protestant theologian of the twentieth century has been Karl Barth (1886-1968). Those who agree and those who disagree with him recognize that he sparked some of the most vigorous Protestant thinking since the Reformation.

Barth's theological transformation began, not in the university, but in the parish. Preaching in the Swiss village of Safenville during the First World War, as he tells us, he needed only a little imagination to hear the guns booming to the north. The platitudes and moralism so common in religion were all too empty for such a time. He heard the New Testament speak to him with its message of salvation. So in 1918 he published his commentary on Paul's letter to the Romans. This was the book that rocked the theological world. It had no dry scholarship, no "objective" reasoning about Christianity. It was an existential declaration of God's holiness, man's sin, Christ's gift of salvation, justification by faith.

Three years later, in a lengthened and revised edition of this book, Barth told of the influence upon him of Kierkegaard and Dostoevsky. Here was the specific impact of existentialism upon a man who was already an existential thinker. Later still, Barth drew back from existentialism. He wanted the biblical message to depend upon no specific philosophy. Further, he feared Kierkegaard's indulgence in introspection and his preoccupation with despair, and chose instead to emphasize the affirmative Gospel, interpreting it in the tradition of the Reformers. (It is only fair to point out that Kierkegaard had himself made the same criticism of existentialism.)

Even if Barth renounced existential*ism,* his writings preserved their existential ring. Late in his career, while emphasizing the objectivity that (as an heir of Calvin) he thought belong in all theology, he acknowledged again his debt to existentialism.[10]

The twentieth century theologian who is generally regarded as an all-out existentialist is Rudolf Bultmann (b. 1884). Taking seriously Kierkegaard's idea of truth as subjectivity, Bultmann worked out a theology that relied heavily on the New Testament, yet depended on almost no objective factual content. His critics argue, rightly or wrongly, that he transforms theology (thought about God) to anthropology (thought about man). In his understanding of man he relies heavily on Heidegger's description of existence. Then he brings to it something lacking in Heidegger, the New Testament *kerygma* (the basic proclamation or the gospel). But he refuses to let that *kerygma* stand in objectivity. Everything depends upon the believer's appropriation and interpretation of it. That means a great emphasis on *hermeneutics,* an old-fashioned word, which has come back into style, for interpretation.

The younger generation of European Christians include a number of post-Bultmanians. The term is used, partly because they modify Bultmann's thinking, partly because in the yen for truly contemporary thinking it has become fashionable to call many movements post-something. The post-Bultmanians (incuding Ernst Fuchs, Gerhard Ebeling, and Heinrich Ott) all emphasize hermeneutics and all draw upon Heidegger's ideas. But whereas Bultmann used the "early" Heidegger's analysis of existence, the post-Bultmanians pay more attention to his later work on language.

In the English-speaking world the two men who played the biggest part in the twentieth century theological reconstruction are, by general consent, Reinhold Niebuhr (b. 1892) and Paul Tillich (1886-1965). Niebuhr's theology, like Barth's was a response to the struggles of faith in the midst of the parish. The effect upon human beings of industrial society in Detroit sent his relentless mind to the Bible and to Augustine, with some attention also to Marx. Later, as he was developing his now-famous doctrine of man, he discovered Kierkegaard. His statements of the gospel are directed to modern society, grappling with the problems of politics, economics, and international hostilities, and to the modern man who is bewildered in the midst of these concerns and in his own struggle for integrity.

Tillich's thought was in some ways more academic, for Tillich was a student of all the great philosophers, including the existentialists. But an army chaplaincy, the struggle against Hitler, migration to a new country, and penetrating interest in psychoanalysis and the arts gave his thought a practical bent. One of his books, *The Courage to Be,* shows considerable influence of Heidegger. But Tillich was very much his own man, and he belonged to nobody's camp. Yet, if we use his own definition of existentialism as thinking in a situation of ultimate concern, he was thoroughly an existentialist. He became an amazingly powerful spokesman to the emptiness and lostness of twentieth-century existence.

Among the generation following Niebuhr and Tillich, most Protestant thinkers have been at least stirred, if not shaken, by existentialism. The most radical existentialist of them all was Carl Michalson, who was rethinking the whole of Christian belief when he lost his life in an airplane crash—another example of the absurd?—at the age of 50. John Macquarrie appropriates some of Heidegger's themes in a reconstruction of theology that is boldly existentialist, yet tempered by Anglican moderation.

Curiously related to existentialism is the situa-

tional ethics that has made a major impact upon
Protestant Christianity. To the extent that Dietrich Bonhoeffer and Karl Barth have contributed
to this ethic, it is existentialist in tone. They insist, with serious reliance upon Scripture, that
Christian ethics is not a matter of finding the
generalizations or rules that can be applied to
particular circumstances. Rather in every situation God faces men with a distinctive requirement
of faithfulness. Thus Bonhoeffer set aside the
commandment against murder because he believed in a particular situation that he should par-
ticipate in a plot aimed to assassinate Hitler. In
their emphasis on the concrete rather than the
abstract, upon the immediacy of ethical decisions,
and on the necessity of taking personal responsibility for decisions that do not fit the rules, the
situationalists are true heirs of Kierkegaard.

But a quite different strain of thought rises in
Joseph Fletcher, the American situationalist."
Fletcher agrees with other situationalists in his
criticism of abstract ethical laws. But his ethic is
in no sense an impulsive one. He puts a great
emphasis on calculation that is very different
from Bonhoeffer and Barth. For Fletcher there is
one absolute good—*agape* or love. Ethics then is a
matter of using an "agapeic calculus"—a reckoning of what action will best fulfill love. Here Fletcher is borrowing and adapting a theme of the
nineteenth century utilitarians, against whom existentialism rebelled. He has changed Bentham's
"hedonistic calculus," an effort to reckon as pre-

cisely as possible the contribution of every act to pleasure or happiness, into an agapeic calculus. Actually the difference is not so great as might appear from the words, since both men are seeking avowedly to maximize happiness.

In recent years some Protestants have objected to the heavy influence on Christian faith of existentialist introspection. Instead of cultivating a hot-house atmosphere of concern about anxiety, they have said Christians should give more attention to the objective political and social problems of the world. Instead of worrying so much about their own sin and salvation, they should show their love for men in worldly action. The fountainhead of this theme was Dietrich Bonhoeffer, whose brave opposition to Hitler led to his death in a concentration camp.

Harvey Cox has stated the case strongly. "Existentialism," he charges, "is the last child of a cultural epoch, born in its mother's senility." Yet Cox also writes that man "doesn't simply discover meaning; he originates it"[12]—an existentialist sentence that comes straight from Nietzsche via Sartre.

The fact is that, as I stated earlier, existentialism is a fractured family. So powerful and pervasive has its influence been on Protestantism that, when someone picks a fight with one branch of the family, he is likely to get his weapons from another branch.

Perhaps that fact is a blessing. The existentialist household is turbulent enough that nobody can settle in for a comfortable stay. In contemporary Protestantism it is hard to be for or against existentialism; it is equally hard to ignore it.

SEVEN
VOICES, SIGHTS, AND DEEDS

AN ALL-OUT EXISTENTIALIST will insist that this
kind of book is a pitiful mistake. (Don't say I didn't
warn you. I brought up the issue on the very first
page of the first chapter.).This book aims to tell
about existentialism, not to be an existentialist
book. It falls fairly neatly into chapters and sections. It simplifies difficult concepts and makes
them seem easier than they are. In all this it
comes close to fraud. One might as well try to
build a scale model of a tiger out of square blocks.

If I agreed completely with that argument, I
would not have written this book. But I readily
agree that no one will get very far into existentialism by reading *about* it. Its adventure of self-discovery forces it to speak with voices of poetry and
drama, to show itself in the visual arts, to live
itself in deeds.

Indirect Communication

Pascal said that he could not write about human
experience in an orderly way, since he was trying
to show that his subject was incapable of order.[1]
And all the great existentialists sooner or later
resort to a kind of deliberate disorder. They prefer
not to lay their theories out neatly before us. They
want to plunge us into the disorder, so that we can
find out for ourselves what they are talking about.

In a whimsical bit of writing Kierkegaard tells
how he decided on his career as an author. In an

outside café one Sunday afternoon he began to think what he might do with his life. He meditated on the great benefactors of mankind, who did so much to make life easier. Then, during his second cigar, an insight flashed upon him. His job would be "to make something harder." So, he said, "I conceive it as my task to create difficulties everywhere."[2] Since then, I think it is fair to say, all existentialists have shared that aim.

The reason is no idiosyncrasy. It is rather what Kierkegaard called the necessity for "indirect communication." The important truths, he says, no one can tell you. Objective facts and reasoned conclusions can be stated directly. But truth that requires self-discovery, truth *for a subject*, cannot be handed from man to man in sentences.

Suppose an artist, for example, explains to you that a certain picture is beautiful. You believe him. You go around repeating the conclusion, "That picture is beautiful." But you do not understand what you are saying unless you personally have discovered the beauty. Similarly the existentialist cannot give you his conclusions. He can at best initiate you—by persuasion or by annoyance —into the experience of discovery.

This experience, carried to the extreme, can end in something like Zen Buddhism. Here the teacher may refuse to tell anything. Instead he asks a question, a *koan* or insoluble riddle. (Example: Two hands when clapped make a sound. What is the sound of one hand clapping?) The koan is meant to be nonsensical, to break the shackles of sense and intellect and thus make illumination possible.

By contrast Christianity offers a clear account, told in Scripture, of the life and teachings of Jesus. Surely that can be told and retold directly. But, says the existentialist (and Kierkegaard in particular), notice the important fact. Christian faith says that the Almighty God meets man in this Jesus. God does not approach man in divine glory and tell man what to think. He comes incognito in a man born in a stable and killed as a criminal. That is God's indirect communication. Men can understand it only if by faith they discover in the persecuted man the savior.

Existentialist literature, therefore, is rarely plain exposition. Kierkegaard used pseudonyms and a variety of literary devices to stir or provoke his readers. Nietzsche used fictitious characters to pronounce his poetic oracles. Other existentialists have written novels, short stories, plays, poetry, literary criticism. Even the most formal of the philosophers break out of strict exposition. Thus Heidegger, who can be pedantic enough, drifts into an ecstatic mood and symbolic language. And Jaspers needs "ciphers" —symbols which point to truth that cannot be stated directly.

The Verbal Arts

Somewhere in the background of most modern existentialism looms the titanic Dostoevsky. Ever since he wrote his turbulent novels, fiction has been a chief form of existentialist expression.

Almost as important as Dostoevsky in the fictional canon is Franz Kafka (1883-1924), the Jewish writer of Prague. Where Dostoevsky wrote of man's violent will, torn between faith and nihilism, Kafka wrote of his bewilderment in a world that lures him to seek its meaning, yet denies him a clear answer. Between the two of them, these novelists do as much to communicate the existentialist mood as all the expository prose ever written on the subject.

More recently an American book reviewer has commented: "Perhaps the dominant literary theme of our century has been that of the terrible loneliness of human beings in a society increasingly diminished in emotional and moral values."[3] Here is evidence that most writers are participating in the existential revolt against the dehumanization of man, in the uncovering of hidden anxiety and despair. Like the philosophers they make their leaps into faith or emptiness.

Usually these writers, like Dostoevsky, do not aim to be existentialists, if they have even heard of that word. And that is itself a decisive fact. No existentialist first thinks up his doctrines, then looks for ways to communicate them. On the contrary, the communication precedes the formal doctrine. For in *activity*—in writing, warring, marrying, praying —persons discover themselves and other selves. The recorded discoveries are literature. Some of this literature self-consciously belongs to existentialism. More often readers recognize themes in the literature and call it existentialist. Among the literary artists usually listed in this movement are Proust, Gide, Malraux, de Beauvoir, Sartre, Camus, and Beckett.

Among American novelists of the past generation the two who dominated literature were William Faulkner and Ernest Hemingway. If Faulkner had been told he was an existentialist, he would have responded with an existential snort. But he knew how to describe the absurd and how to ask bewildering questions about the place of man in the universe. Sartre, though taking Faulkner very seriously, objects that Faulkner does not understand the importance of time and freedom. Camus, who liked Faulkner more than did Sartre, translated him into French and gave him a wide audience.

Hemingway also belongs to the story, not because of his ability to tell a rattling good story—few existentialists do that sort of thing—but because of his fictional brooding over the meaning of existence. He was as fascinated as Heidegger with "nothing"—and more gloomy about it. The oppressiveness of his feelings come out in his rewriting of the Lord's Prayer in one of his short stories, "A Clean, Well-Lighted Place." Using *nada,* the Spanish word for nothing, one of his characters says: "Our nada who art in nada, nada be thy name" . . . and so on.

In the current generation of American novelists Norman Mailer is one who does not hesitate to use the term existentialism. John Updike, a serious

reader of Pascal and Kierkegaard, writes powerfully of sin and frustration and intimations of
grace. A host of lesser writers interrogate man's
inner experience with questions that are prominent in the existentialist tradition.

The most famous of the deliberately existentialist novelists is Sartre. Like Kierkegaard, he ex-
poses the irrationalities and hypocrisies of life.
But his method is different. Often he concen-
trates, to the point of an obsession, upon the sor-
did, the obscene, the sexually abnormal. His use of
sex, however, has no similarity to the efforts at
titillation of so many gaudy paperbacks on the
newsstands (even though some of his books have
been on the stands). Rather, he is uncovering the
despair and revulsion of meaningless lives, and
the possibility of some kind of authentic self-affir-
mation.

Very different, as we have already seen, is Albert Camus. He is almost a theologian who disbelieves in God, a man so thirsty for divinity that
he resents God for not existing. His themes are
familiar Christian ones: the decision to join the
innocent sufferers rather than the sinful conquer-
ors, the torments of the guilty conscience, the
pained cry for redemption. He shows us tragic
characters who can at least glimpse heroic nobil-
ity. He almost says, "My God, my God, why hast
thou forsaken me?" He cannot say, "Father, into
thy hands I commend my spirit."

Even more than fiction, poetry communicates
indirectly. A genuine poem—I am excluding prose

that happens to have rhyme and meter—conveys
more than it says literally. It requires a peculiar
concentration of the listener, who must let himself be drawn into the world of the poet, there to
discover what the poet cannot say baldly. In this
broad sense, poetry is inevitably existential. The
sensitive imagination of the poet often beats the
philosopher to existential insights. Thus Robert
Frost, whose sturdy New England spirit was
remote from the seething atmosphere of most existentialism, nevertheless expressed existential
yearnings and forebodings profoundly. When Lio-
nel Trilling once said as much, Frost's enthusiasts
rushed to defend him as the All-American poet.
But Trilling's evidence stood.

Other poets stand more specifically in the existentialist tradition. Two great Germans, Hölder-
lin (1770-1843) and Rilke (1875-1926), have
become almost patron saints of existentialism,
partly because Heidegger has given them concentrated attention.

Among the English-language poets are many
who belong to this story. Perhaps the most notable
are T. S. Eliot and W. H. Auden, the American-
turned-Englishman and the Englishman-turned-
American. Both moved from skepticism to
Christian faith. Eliot's manners of an English gen-
tleman and his formal Anglo-Catholicism were
radically offensive to many rebellious existentialists; yet he fascinated them when he probed the
emptiness and shattered the false fronts of modern culture. Auden, familiar with the haunts and

the language both of secularists and of churchmen, often expresses existentialism in deft verse.
Both poets know how to combine flashing wit and
deep reverence. It is no accident that Eliot wrote
an introduction to Pascal's *Pensées* and that
Auden edited a book of selections from Kierkegaard.

A host of younger poets are carrying out their
own rebellions against the established forms and
content of poetry. The recovery of poetry on the
college campuses, in an era when poetry had
pretty much been put on the shelf, is a notable
fact of our time. The poetry that "gets through"
these days is largely the poetry that seeks to express personal authenticity. If some of the poets
need to be reminded that it is as tempting to fake
authenticity as to fake respectability, the better
ones are fully aware of that trap.[4]

The Theater

In a way all drama, except pure spectacle and
amusement, is existential. The power of the stage,
whether in comedy or tragedy, is to draw its audience into its action. By engaging people in dramatic conflict it stirs them to awareness of
themselves and their world.

More particularly the American theater from
Eugene O'Neill onward has concentrated on existentialist themes. Usually the stimulus has not
been philosophy or theology. More often the im-
petus has come from the history of our time, from

the Marxist and Freudian affronts to old ways, from shattering wars and inner disturbances.

The common complaint against the contemporary theater is that it is not pleasant. It is more likely to be ugly or sublime than "pretty." Just that complaint is a tribute to the implicit existentialism of our foremost playwrights.

More explicitly existentialist are the plays of Sartre. *No Exit,* for example, offers a fascinating mixture of Christian and atheistic themes. The setting is a room located (as the audience soon discovers) in Hell. Three characters are lodged there. Garcin, editor of a pacifist paper, has treated his wife shabbily and (contrary to his own dreams) has died a coward's death. Estelle, a nymphomaniac, has married for money, chased many men, and killed her illegitimate baby. Inez, a lesbian, has ruined the lives of several people.

The three gradually realize that they are doomed to torment each other forever. Hell, they conclude, is "other people." Yet, at the dramatic moment when the door flies open, no one can leave. Each *needs* the others whom he so hates.

Repeatedly the characters see possibilities of hope. In a series of *ifs,* they confess their plight. If they could *trust* or have *faith* in each other, show some *human feeling* of sympathy, *convince* each other, then *love* would be possible. They could be *saved.* But their Hell has *No Exit.*

The play is a dramatic essay on the New Testament doctrine of salvation by grace and justification by faith. But there is no grace and no faith.

Kierkegaard has left his mark on Sartre, but Sartre refuses to join Kierkegaard in his leap.

Several gifted playwrights—notably Samuel Beckett, Eugene Ionesco, Jean Genet, Harold Pinter, and Friedrich Dürrenmatt—have dramatized existentialist themes. Out of their work has come the "theater of the absurd." Obviously a play may be absurd simply because its writer lacks wit or concentration, and there is plenty of such absurdity in the theater. But a writer of real wit and concentration may do a play that is absurd in the sense that Kierkegaard and Camus used that word. Then it is existentialist in thrust.

The theater shows other marks of the existentialist posture: "the method," which requires actors to feel their way emotionally into their roles; the increased tendency to involve the audience in the play; and the movement from the carefully planned play to "the happening." Since acting is a skill, since even the classical theater in some real sense "involved" the audience, and since not all that happens is art, these new theatrical trends prompt questions. Given the nature of our times, the questions are not likely to be answered definitively very soon.

The new burst of imagination in the cinema is also part of the existentialist story. Since motion pictures can break loose from some of the restrictions of the stage, there has been something of a shift of creativity from the theater to the cinema in recent years. Such producers as Ingmar Bergman, Federico Fellini, Luis Bunuel, and Jean-Luc

Godard know how to rub raw the nerve of existence and expose its absurdities; sometimes they know how to see glimmers of meaning and affirmations of confidence in the midst of frustration. They are intrigued with religious symbols and use them powerfully, sometimes in deliberate parody, sometimes in ways that leave the viewer to decide what he must make of them.

The Visual Arts and Music

Only artists, said Nietzsche, "dare to show us the human being as he is." The artist searches out the unique self which others cover up.

Look, for instance, at the "portraits" made by conventional photographers. Careful retouching eliminates wrinkles and blemishes so as to give all faces a pasty uniformity. The photographer aims to show, not a self, but a mask—the more like other masks, the better. When the masks get too monotonously alike, he tries a trick camera angle, which far from showing the real person simply produces an *uncharacteristic* (characterless) pose. Anyone who stubbornly demands an unretouched photograph seems a little crazy. If his picture gets into the newspaper, he looks like a thug. People are so used to artificiality that the real appears false.

By contrast an artist (not just any commercial portrait-painter) aims to show the real person. A Rembrandt portrait, for example, depicts an honest self, not likely to be confused with the masks on the society page of the newspaper. In this concern for selfhood, all art has an existential quality.

But now comes a special development that delights or infuriates people. Although it has a long history, it has been exploited peculiarly in contemporary art. It is the artist's deliberate distortion of his subject-matter. It may appear arbitrary, but it has its reason. The famous painter, Paul Klee, explains: "Art does not reproduce the visible; rather, it makes visible." Why should the artist go to the trouble of showing what anybody can see without him? He aims to get behind the surface, to disclose the hidden depths of things. And he communicates indirectly. Take his picture as direct portrayal, and it looks false. Take it on its own terms, and it suggests or wakens a new discovery.

In some of Van Gogh's landscapes the brilliant colors, the bold splotches of paint, the swirling brushstrokes look like nothing anyone ever saw. The artist is not aiming to give an *objective* picture of nature; scientists and photographers can do that. He is making an *existential* painting (though he probably never heard the word). He is showing what a scene means to *him.* He is disclosing the hidden vitality and turbulence of nature —and, no doubt, of his own spirit.

Van Gogh's paintings are still recognizably landscapes and people. More recent art may show no such resemblance at all—or a resemblance that somehow "dawns" on one. Picasso, for example, reveals the hidden beauty in ugliness and the hidden ugliness in beauty. He reaches past appearance for the inner dynamics of life or things. He is not satisfied that the viewer should observe. He wants to draw him out, "engage" him, show him something by awakening in him the capability of seeing it.

I am not trying to say that contemporary art is good. Some is grand, some merely grandiose. Some is revealing, some just confused. What I am saying is that a large part of today's art is existential.

The most powerful of recent Christian painters was Georges Rouault. Nobody calls his works lovely or nice. He does not please so much as he shatters. In one painting of Christ he can show more of suffering majesty than comes through in ten years of religious calendar art. Christian existentialism tells us that the church has too often been duped by art that seemed religious, because it pictured Jesus of the three wise men, but which was actually irreligious in its flabbiness.[5] I can only add a brief note on music. In one sense music is the most existential of the arts, because no words or pictures define its content. Its meaning is largely the meaning which the listener gives it. For the same reason music is not likely to express a *specific* existentialism.

Yet there is a peculiarly modern existential mode in music. William Barrett finds it in Beethoven's last quartets, where "the dissolution of accepted musical form" sounds "the dissolution of a whole world of accepted status."[6] Others find it in the rhythms and improvisations of jazz. Still others find it in the new scales and dissonances of contemporary experimentalists.

As with the visual arts, some of this music is superb, some wretched. I can run as fast as the next man from the juke box. I am only pointing to a quality of uneasiness, rebellion against classical forms, perhaps loneliness and anxiety in some contemporary music, good and bad. The devotee of jazz, of rock and roll, or of folk music does not say, "That's a pretty number"; he may say, "It sends me." And that just might mean, "It's existential."

Tamed Existentialism

The same existentialism which pervades the arts operates in more hard-boiled and more prosaic areas of life. The real existentialist cannot separate thought from action. He may, like Kierkegaard, seek to reform a church or, like André Malraux, lay aside his research to take a place in General De Gaulle's government.

In American society the widest diffusion of existential ideas has come—surprising as it may seem —through pragmatism. William James, the pioneer pragmatist, knew the spell of Pascal. But his philosophy was genuinely homegrown. Not by reading European existentialists but by confronting American situations he came to assert the role of man's will in the perception of truth, the urgency of activity and decision.

John Dewey, many will say, surely rooted out any existentialist weeds in the pragmatist's garden. True, Dewey's insistence on scientific method as the sole way to truth opposed the main thrust of existentialism. Yet Dewey's early writings expressed both the kinship and alienation between man and his universe in terms that had existential overtones. And he was always the enemy of rational systems which cramped the variety of experience. Even logic, insisted Dewey, can never be a purely abstract system, because thinking always takes place in an "existential matrix."[7] Man is no pure mind; he thinks in order to meet problems of his biological and cultural existence. But Dewey's description of existence drew nothing from the major existentialists. It was more characteristic of an age of progress than an "Age of Anxiety."[8]

Dewey was for years the foremost influence on American "progressive education." In its insistence on the relation between thought and action in learning, it represented one existentialist theme. Its emphasis on self-expression has some relation to the existentialist cry for freedom of the unique personality. More recently it has given so much attention to social adjustment in education that critics like David Riesman[9] wonder whether it is stifling the personal development it set out to encourage.

A strain of wildness is so characteristic of existentialism that the tamed version in American pragmatism and education should not be called existentialism. But the stormwinds that occasionally blow through American public education are fringes of the tornado that has rocked vast sections of the modern world.

A New Age of Protest

Hard as it is to believe today, as recently as 1957 an exhaustive survey of sociological studies of American college students described these students as "gloriously contented" and "dutifully responsive toward government."[10] The standard complaint of commencement speakers and journalists was that students were conformists with no aim except to find their comfortable place in the affluent society.

But there were signs missed by the sociological surveys. Kenneth Rexroth looked at the art of the "beat generation" and the "beatniks" and decided: "The youngest generation is in a state of revolt so absolute that its elders cannot even recognize it. The disaffiliation, alienation, and rejection of the young has, as far as their elders are concerned, moved out of the visible spectrum altogether."[11] Apparently the sociological surveys concentrated on the visible spectrum and missed some of the most important things going on.

Before long, the protest surfaced as a worldwide rebellion of youth. This does not mean that all youth rebelled; it means that youth all over the world rebelled. The rebellion made its target "the establishment"—whether of government, education, church, or culture. And the rebellion took two rather different forms.

One form was disengagement and withdrawal from the rituals and responsibilities that are dear to the establishment. The hippies, for the most part, did not bother to protest against going institutions or try to reform them; they simply checked out.

Inevitably there were elements of a fad in the hippie rebellion. It is hard to avoid conformity, and the international hippie uniform became as recognizable in North America, Europe, and Asia as the international business man's uniform. But the hippies were living out their complaint against organization, bureaucracy, and a technological world that they found, in a favorite word, dehumanizing. They wanted to be human, to do their own thing—individually or in small groups where they could find an experience of community that established institutions quashed.

Much of this is characteristic of the existentialist posture. To the extent that the hippies rely upon drugs for experience of selfhood, they would seem to be practicing the fallacy that they attack —using mechanical means for an end that can only be achieved personally. And to the extent that they renounce responsibility, they deny the existentialist insistence on involvement. But in seeing the enemy as the depersonalized system and in trying to claim personal authenticity, they are existentialist through and through.

The second form of the rebellion meant positive protest and direct action against social wrongs. This protest called for involvement—in civil rights movements, in black power, in anti-war efforts. It too objected to the dehumanizing forces of our world. In its claiming of responsibility and its insistence upon action based on decision, it was thoroughly existentialist.

Since its goals required political action, it faced a problem that has often haunted existentialism: how do you reconcile individual authenticity with the demands of the political process. Politics is not simply doing your own thing; it is organization, discipline negotiation, compromise. The cry for involvement drove the protesters into the political processes that, by their own testimony, thwarted personal authenticity.

The answer was a call for a "new politics" to replace the old cynical politics with its wheeling-and-dealing. The new left arose out of existential, sometimes existentialist concern for human problems. It has awakened new political impulses in our society. Its problem—the problem of Norman Mailer when he ran for mayor of New York and the problem of the idealists seeking peace and racial justice—is whether they can make their aims programmatic without losing the human authenticity that set them on their way.

It should be evident that the hippies and the new left, in some ways quite different from each other, face similar problems. The hippy by conviction probably cannot become a soldier. But if he really believes in peace, he may be moved to try to modify national policy. That puts him in the middle of the political problem, perhaps beside the new leftist. The two have trouble communicating, but they find that they can communicate better with each other than with the establishment. So they may make common cause.

Existentialists have usually not been very good at politics. Kierkegaard would have been as ill at ease in politics, had he tried it, as he was in the church of his time. Heidegger made an awful gaffe in his misjudgment of the Nazis. Sartre was brilliant in the French resistance, when opposition was itself action, but in later years he did not know what to do except to try to relate clumsily to the French communists. Politics remains strange terrain for existentialist personalism. Yet existentialist purposes frequently run into frustration on political problems. Conceivably a new generation can learn to operate in this realm without losing existentialist resolve and personal authenticity. The evidence is not yet in.

EIGHT
SOME EXISTENTIAL JUDGMENTS

THERE IS NO SENSE IN CASTING a vote for or against existentialism. That would be like voting for or against the wind. Winds save crops and cleanse cities; they also rip apart barns and factories. Existentialism likewise brings blessings and fury.

Neither can a critic give a cool, objective appraisal of existentialism. He might try to point out, impartially of course, just what is good and bad about it. But if he attempts *that,* the joke is on him; for if there is *any* truth in existentialism, no one can carry off such a pose. The critic is himself a struggling person, haunted by anxieties, lured by goals beyond his attainment. He does not sit in majesty above the strife; he is in the midst of it. His judgment about existentialism is itself an existential judgment. He may—and should — appeal to facts and logic, but he will reason from the point of view of his own despair and hope, his faith and unfaith.

Realizing all this, I shall state some of my judgments on existentialism. In doing so, I am simply putting directly the views that have already influenced every page of this book.

The greatest contribution of existentialism has been to recover a posture that is characteristic of most great philosophy and of the Bible. When history conspired against man to deny him this posture, the explosive breakthrough came. It brought its glories and its excesses, its magnificence and

its depravity. It is a grand and fearful achievement. It declares to all who are capable of hearing
that there can be no personal living and certainly
no Christianity that are not existential. Without
courage, without concern, without commitment
life is hollow.

The specific teachings of contemporary existentialism are more varied and more debatable. Some
of these have a mighty value for our time. Often
they are unpleasant. They strip the glittering
chrome and cellophane from this marvelous civilization and expose some harsh realities.

Existentialism tells us of brutal contradictions
in our society. The public creed praises personal
freedom; but poverty and prejudice deny opportunity to some, and prosperity lures others to
scrap selfhood and love in the rat race for wealth.
Advertising promises to sell happiness to people,
who try by buying to bury anxieties that will not
stay buried. Industry and construction give the
illusion of permanence to cities that may blow up
in world destruction any month. Churches talk
about God; but popular religion makes people
comfortable where they are instead of leading
them to divine judgment and grace.

When so much security is phony, when happiness is a fraud, when religion deals with illusions,
existentialism is a call to reality. It asks man to
discover himself, to face his world, to meet his
destiny. In calling people to these tasks which
they would rather avoid, it shows them a way to
health.

Existentialism has its dangers, too. They are partly the dangers of courageous adventure, partly the dangers of foolishness. It is not easy to separate the two, for each danger is closely related to a major strength.

1. In rejecting mediocrity and conformity, existentialism easily becomes a pose. Its history and vocabulary lend themselves to faddism. Rebels and nonconformists are easy game for cults. The attack on everything phony readily turns into a stunt as phony as any other. In some types of existentialism, Will Herberg says, "the forlornness and despair of existence are strangely transmuted into a kind of self-satisfied, rather cozy, defiance of the universe."[1] The person of profound convictions often lives in heroic nonconformity; but the person who sets out to be a nonconformist is less a hero than a clown.

2. The thirst for freedom and selfhood can readily degenerate into theatrical self-assertion. "Be yourself," say the existentialists. But which self shall I be? The self that finds its freedom in deep loyalties, or the self that seeks freedom from loyalty?

Here is one of the sharpest differences between atheistic and Christian existentialists. The atheist rejects God, for God might inhibit his freedom. The Christian prays in traditional words, "O God whose service is perfect freedom. . . . " The atheist seeks freedom in self-expression, the Christian, in death to sin and resurrection to new life. The atheist says—rightly—that much talk of Christian freedom is just a veil for a life of subservience to imposed codes. The Christian says—rightly—that the atheistic existentialists have not yet investigated the great teachings of Christian freedom.

3. Existentialism, emphasizing the importance of personal decision, sometimes says, in effect: "Just decide. It doesn't matter what you decide, if the decision is yours." It has no use for the person who gives up his power of decision, and so it refuses to give ethical advice.

The trouble is that even the most personal decision has some moral context and looks to some guiding loyalty. When existentialism refuses any such help, another allegiance fills the vacuum. Thus in the Hitler epoch Heidegger for a time supported the Nazis and Sartre fought against them—not in spite of their existentialism (as some churchmen fought against each other in spite of their faith) but as an expression of the commitment that constituted the existentialist ethic. Somehow existentialism must learn, without handing the individual will over to external authority, to subject that will to moral judgment.

4. In showing the unique quality of personality, which must not be swamped in any social mass, the existentialists have often failed to realize that no one becomes a self except in human relations. Society is as much a part of selfhood as individuality. Buber, Marcel, and Jaspers have seen this

point; Camus came to appreciate it. There are signs that Sartre is catching on. But the existentialist tradition has been largely unrealistic in its individualism.

Thus Christian existentialism sometimes lacks a "social gospel." It has the essential foundation for one: the recognition that Christian faith is radically different from the popular blasphemies which assume that God just naturally approves everything American and hates everything Russian. And in its penetrating view of what society is doing to persons, it shows signs of developing a "social gospel" richer than some past ones. But much of that job is still ahead.

Similarly Christian existentialism often does not know what to make of the church. Seeing the hypocrisies and compromises within the church, it sometimes calls the individual from the church to lonely faith in God. Like the biblical prophets, it sees that God must condemn much that is done in his name. But often it fails to see that Christian faith demands Christian community. It forgets that the church, despite its failings, transmits the Scriptures, celebrates the sacraments, and introduces new generations into the very Christian faith that rightly makes them critical of the church.

5. Sometimes the existentialist does not know how to distinguish between "I feel" and "I believe." He rightly sees that truth-in-barren-objectivity will not do much for anyone, that only

truth-inwardly-appropriated can disturb and heal. But in shifting his focus from knowledge to the knower, he may almost forget the long cosmic and human history that precedes every person and sets many of the conditions of life.

The Christian existentialist knows well the faith that outleaps all reason. He sometimes forgets that human reason, limited and clouded though it is, has a kinship to the divine Logos—the Word and Reason of God, who corrects and illumines our reason, but does not destroy it. And insisting on the necessity of the "leap of faith," he sometimes makes it more of a lurch into the dark than it is. Faith, as Paul Tillich says, is not so much a *grasping* as a *being grasped.* Pascal represents Christ as saying: "Thou wouldst not seek Me, if Thou didst not possess Me."[2] The Christian leaps across the chasm toward God because God has already crossed that chasm to meet men.

So existentialism—whether atheistic or God-directed in Jewish, Christian, or yet other ways — is full of problems. But it is grappling with those problems, testing its wit and its muscle on them. All in all, it is the most stimulating and disturbing, the most bewildering and illuminating movement of thought in a good many generations.

And yet, no one should take the advice to go out and become an existentialist. Kierkegaard, the pioneer, never aimed to be an existentialist. He just tried to be an honest man. And that is a good idea for everyone.

NOTES BY CHAPTERS

CHAPTER TWO

1. Martin Luther, Lecture on Psalm 5, Weimar edition of Luther's Works, V, 183.

CHAPTER THREE

1. René Descartes, *Meditations*, No. 2.
2. Blaise Pascal, *Pensées* (New York: E. P. Dutton & Co., Inc., 1908), fr. [fragments] 205, 206, respectively.
3. *Ibid.*, fr. 277.
4. *Ibid.*, fr. 919.
5. See *The Short Novels of Dostoevsky*, tr. by Constance Garnett (New York: Dial Press, Inc., 1951).
6. Quoted by Rollo May, *The Springs of Creative Living* (Nashville: Abingdon-Cokesbury Press, 1940), p. 30.

CHAPTER FOUR

1. H. Richard Niebuhr, "Sören Kierkegaard," in *Christianity and the Existentialists*, Carl Michalson, ed. (New York: Charles Scribner's Sons, 1956), pp. 27-28.
2. Quoted by Radaslov Tsanoff, *The Great Philosophers* (New York: Harper & Row, 1953), p. 417.
3. *Pensées, op. cit.*, fr. 272.
4. Sören Kierkegaard, *Concluding Unscientific Postscript*, tr. by David F. Swenson and Walter Lowrie (Princeton: Princeton University Press, 1944), p. 174.
5. *Ibid.*, title of Book II, Part Two, Chapter II.
6. Sören Kierkegaard, *Training in Christianity*, tr. by Walter Lowrie (Princeton: Princeton University Press, 1944), p. 87.
7. *Concluding Unscientific Postscript, op. cit.*, p. 179.
8. *Ibid.*, p. 485.
9. *Ibid.*, pp. 179-180.
10. Sören Kierkegaard, *Purity of Heart Is to Will One Thing* (New York: Harper & Row, 1938), pp. 35-36.
11. The quoted phrase is the title of Kierkegaard's famous book describing anxiety.

12. *Concluding Unscientific Postscript, op. cit.*, p. 105.
13. *Training in Christianity, op. cit.*, Kierkegaard's own favorite among his books, is a meditation on this text from Matthew 11:28.
14. *Training in Christianity, op. cit.*, p. 89. *Fear and Trembling* is the title of another of Kierkegaard's books.
15. Kierkegaard's *Attack upon "Christendom,"* tr. by Walter Lowrie (Princeton: Princeton University Press, 1944), p. 20.
16. *Training in Christianity, op. cit.,* p. 39.
17. *The Journals of Kierkegaard*, tr. by Alexander Dru (New York: Oxford University Press, 1938), Entry 1102.

CHAPTER FIVE
1. Carl Michalson, ed., *Christianity and the Existentialists, op. cit.*, p. 20.
2. Friedrich Nietzsche, *The Joyful Wisdom*, tr. by Thomas Common (New York: The Macmillan Company, 1910), Section 125.
3. See Thomas J. J. Altizer and William Hamilton, *Radical Theology and the Death of God*, (Indianapolis: The Bobbs-Merrill Company, Inc., 1966).
4. Jean-Paul Sartre, *The Words* (Greenwich, Conn.: Fawcett Publication, Inc., 1964), p. 157.
5. *Ibid.*, p. 158.
6. Jean-Paul Sartre, "Existentialism," in *Existentialism from Dostoevsky to Sartre*, Walter Kaufmann, ed. (New York: Meridian Books, 1956), p. 3ll.
7. Martin Heidegger, *What is Called Thinking?* (New York: Harper & Row, 1968), p. 244.
8. Jacques Maritain, *The Range of Reason* (New York: Charles Scribner's Sons, 1952).
9. *Christianity and the Existentialists, op. cit.*, p. 21.

CHAPTER SIX
1. Encyclical *Humani Generis*, issued August 21, 1950.
2. Christopher Dawson, *Religion and Culture* (London: Sheed and Ward, Ltd., 1948).
3. Jacques Maritain, *Existence and the Existent* (Garden City, N. Y.: Doubleday Image, 1956), pp. 15-69, 79, 129-141, 148-153.
4. The title of a two-volume work by Gabriel Marcel (Chicago: Henry Regnery Company, 1950, 1951).
5. Martin Buber, *Between Man and Man* (Boston: Beacon Press, 1955), pp. 81-82.
6. Martin Buber, *I and Thou* (Edinburgh: T. & T. Clark, 1937), p. 52.
7. *Ibid.*, pp. 18, 11.

8. *Ibid.*, p. 34.
9. Will Herberg, ed., *Four Existentialist Theologians* (Garden City, N. Y.: Doubleday Anchor, 1958), p. 20.
10. Karl Barth, *The Humanity of God* (Richmond, Va.: John Knox Press, 1960), pp. 56-57.
11. Joseph Fletcher, *Situation Ethics* (Philadelphia: Westminster Press, 1966).
12. Harvey Cox, *The Secular City* (New York: The Macmillan Co., 1965), pp. 252, 74.

CHAPTER SEVEN

1. *Pensées, op. cit.*, fr. 373.
2. *Concluding Unscientific Postscript, op. cit.*, pp. 164-165.
3. William Peden, *New York Times Book Review*, June 22, 1958, p. 18.
4. For a more profound and extended review of existentialism in fiction and poetry, see Stanley Romaine Hopper, "The Author in Search of His Anecdote," in *Restless Adventure: Essays on Contemporary Expressions of Existentialism*, edited by Roger L. Shinn (New York: Charles Scribner's Sons, 1968).
5. See Paul Tillich, "Existentialist Aspects of Modern Art," in *Christianity and the Existentialists*, Carl Michalson, ed., *op. cit*
6. William Barrett, *What Is Existentialism?* (New York: Partisan Review Pamphlet, 1947), p. 54.
7. John Dewey, *Logic: the Theory of Inquiry* (New York: Henry Holt and Company, Inc., 1938), Chs. 2-3.
8. The title of a book-length poem by W. H. Auden (New York: Random House, Inc., 1947).
9. David Riesman *et al., The Lonely Crowd* (Garden City, N. Y.: Doubleday Anchor, 1953), pp. 76-85.
10. Philip Jacob, *Changing Values in College* (New York: Harper & Row, 1957), pp. 1, 2.
11. Kenneth Rexroth, "Disengagement: The Art of the Beat Generation," in *The Beat Generation and the Angry Young Men* (New York: Dell Publishing Company, Inc., 1959), p. 351. This essay was earlier published in *New World Writing,* No. 11, 1957.

CHAPTER EIGHT

1. Will Herberg, *Judaism and Modern Man* (New York: Farrar, Straus and Young, 1951), p. 31.
2. *Pensées, op. cit.*, fr. 554.

FOR FURTHER READING

FOR FURTHER READING

Writings of the Existentialists

The best place to start is with some books by the great existentialists. This list includes only authors who have been discussed above and books which are available in popular, paperback editions.

Martin Buber, *I and Thou,* second edition (New York: Charles Scribner's Sons, 1958).

—. *Between Man and Man* (Boston: Beacon Press, 1955).

—. *Eclipse of God* (New York: Harper & Row Torchbooks, 1957).

Albert Camus, *The Stranger* (New York: Vintage Books, 1954).

—. *The Myth of Sisyphus* (New York: Vintage Books, 1955). These two books, a novel and an essay, are Camus' description of "the absurd."

—. *The Plague* (New York: Modern Library, 1958).

—. *The Rebel* (New York: Vintage Books, 1956).

These two books, also a novel and an essay, express the "tragic humanism" of Camus.

—. *The Fall* (New York: Vintage Books, 1956).

—. *Exile and the Kingdom* (New York: Vintage Books, 1958). These books, both fiction, are from the final period of Camus' life.

Will Herberg, ed., *Four Existentialist Theologians* (Garden City, N. Y.: Doubleday Anchor, 1958). Selections from Berdyaev, Buber, Maritain, Tillich, with helpful introductions.

Karl Jaspers, *Man in the Modern Age* (Garden City, N. Y.: Doubleday Anchor, 1957). A discussion of contemporary civilization with its threats to personality.

—. *Reason and Existenz* (New York: Noonday Press, 1957). Comments on Kierkegaard and Nietzsche, followed by a discussion of metaphysics and communication.

Frederick R. Karl and Leo Hamalian, eds., *The Existential Imagination* (Greenwich, Conn.: Fawcett Premier Books, 1963). Selected readings in fiction and drama from Shakespeare to the present.

Walter Kaufman, ed., *Existentialism from Dostoevsky to Sartre* (NewYork: Meridian Books, 1956). A very useful collection of writings from Kierkegaard, Nietzsche, Kafka, Heidegger, and others, with introductions.

Sören Kierkegaard, *Fear and Trembling* and *The Sickness unto Death* (Garden City, N. Y.: Doubleday Anchor, 1954). Two short books, bound together, which explore anxiety and faith in the manner which set the style for many later existentialists.

—. *Either-Or* (Garden City, N. Y.: Doubleday Anchor, 1959). A long book for serious readers.

—. *Philosophical Fragments* (Princeton, N. J.: Princeton University Press, 1962).

—. *Concluding Unscientific Postscript* (Princeton, N. J.: Princeton University Press, 1941). The two preceding books are a pair, giving Kierkegaard's philosophical argument. They require concentration.

—. *Training in Christianity* (Princeton, N. J.: Princeton University Press, 1944). Kierkegaard's Christian faith. His favorite among his books.

—. *Attack upon "Christendom"* (Boston: Beacon Press, 1965). The scathing, witty writings that I have described, very inadequately, in his book.

Gabriel Marcel, *The Philosophy of Existentialism* (New York: Citadel Press, 1961). Marcel's statement of his own philosophy and his criticism of Sartre.

Jean-Paul Sartre, *No Exit and Three Other Plays* (New York: Vintage Books, 1955). The most entertaining and perhaps the best way into Sartre's "atheistic existentialism."

—. *Intimacy and other Short Stories* (New York: Avon, 1948). Another way to enter Sartre. The short stories are not as good as the plays except for two classics, "The Wall" and "The Childhood of a Leader."

—. *Being and Nothingness*, abridged ed., (New York: Citadel, 1966). The major philosophical work in English thus far. For serious students.

—. *The Words* (Greenwich, Conn.: Fawcett Crest Book, 1966). The first volume of Sartre's autobiography. Other volumes are on the way.

William V. Spanos, ed., *A Casebook on Existentialism* (New York: Thomas Y. Crowell, 1966). Readings from existentialist writers in three classifications: literature, commentary and criticism, philosophy and theology.

Paul Tillich, *The Dynamics of Faith* (New York: Harper & Row Torchbooks, 1958). A description of faith as "ultimate concern" by a great Protestant philosopher-theologian.

Writings About Existentialism

Of the many books about existentialism, these few may be the best for following up the themes of this book. This list has to reach outside the paperbacks.

William Barrett, *Irrational Man: A Study in Existential Philosophy* (Garden City, N. Y.: Doubleday Anchor, 1958). A description by an able and perceptive philosopher at New York University.

Robert Bretall, ed., *A Kierkegaard Anthology* (Princeton: Princeton University Press, 1946). An excellent way to get into Kierkegaard. The selections are arranged in chronological order, matched with excerpts from the *Journals*, and introduced by helpful comments from the editor.

F. H. Heinemann, *Existentialism and the Modern Predicament* (New York: Harper & Row Torchbooks, 1958). An exposition by one of the participants in European existentialism.

Walter Lowrie, *A Short Life of Kierkegaard* (Princeton: Princeton University Press, 1942; paperback ed., 1958). An excellent biography by a pioneer translator of Kierkegaard.

Carl Michalson, ed., *Christianity and the Existentialists* (New York: Charles Scribner's Sons, 1956). A collection of lectures on famous existentialists by H. Richard Niebuhr, Paul Tillich, and others.

Roger L. Shinn, ed., *Restless Adventure: Essays on Contemporary Expressions of Existentialism* (New York: Charles Scribner's Sons, 1968). Five writers describe existentialism in philosophy, theology, literature, art, and psychology.